From the Farm to the Pharmacist and Beyond

From the Farm to the Pharmacist and Beyond

✦

What a man does for himself will die with him. What a man does for others will live forever.

Bill Haithco, R.Ph.

iUniverse, Inc.
New York Lincoln Shanghai

From the Farm to the Pharmacist and Beyond
What a man does for himself will die with him. What a man does for others will live forever.

iUniverse books may be ordered through booksellers or by contacting:

iUniverse
2021 Pine Lake Road, Suite 100
Lincoln, NE 68512
www.iuniverse.com
1-800-Authors (1-800-288-4677)

Because of the dynamic nature of the Internet, any Web addresses or links contained in this book may have changed since publication and may no longer be valid.

The views expressed in this work are solely those of the author and do not necessarily reflect the views of the publisher, and the publisher hereby disclaims any responsibility for them.

ISBN: 978-0-595-43865-5 (pbk)
ISBN: 978-0-595-88188-8 (ebk)

Printed in the United States of America

Dedicated to:

My Grandchildren

Danielle Elyse Haithco

William H. Haithco, III

Jai Spencer Haithco, II

REV.JAI,BILLY,DANIELLE,WILLIAM III,DAD, SHARI

Special Thanks to Kim Maul,

Hope, Michigan

without whose guidance this book would not be published.

Also special thanks to

William H. Haithco, II, Technical Consultant
Shari Clarke, Clerical Assistant
Rev. Jai S. Haithco, Spiritual Assistant
Beatrice Green

In Honor of:

Brother Attorney Horace J. Rodgers

and

Brother Leon Allain (deceased)

"You paddled me across the burning sands.

I have not winced nor cried aloud!"

In Honor of:

The Founders of Gamma Tau Chapter
Alpha Phi Alpha Fraternity
Michigan State University

With the foundations of fraternity organization and policy securely laid, the attention of the founders turned to expansion. Recognizing the fact that there had been developed, at Cornell University, an organization of unusual merit and unique character among black college men, it was only natural that the concept of Alpha Phi Alpha should turn toward other colleges and universities, in which there were students in need of the same fellowship advantages.

Carl Armstrong, Herbert Burnett, Alvis Caleman, Clarence C. Gray, Frederick Johnson, William Haithco, Calvin Sharpe (deceased), William H. Thompson, Thomas Walker, amd Bill Richardson (deceased), saw reason to promote real fraternal brotherhood and founded Gamma Tau chapter on May 1, 1948 at Michigan State University. More objectives of the chapter have been to stimulate an understanding of and appreciation for our place in domestic affairs, both as a fraternity and as a people.

We take true pride in saying, "We're the brothers of Gamma Tau chapter"!

Bro. Michael Blackman

"My head is bloody but unbowed."

Contents

Introduction

"I would like to do research in the Great Barrier Reef ... but I cannot swim."
"To thine own self be true and thou cannot be false to any man."
"Be yourself as no one is better qualified."

I was the first black Registered Pharmacist in the history of Saginaw, Michigan, but I have never seen it recorded in "history". Since local historians were mainly white, they mainly wrote history of "whites". History is not always accurate.

I cannot recall any of the old non-white citizens writing the history of the blacks in Saginaw County, Michigan, and their accomplishments. Some have called me rather recently asking my help in compiling such history. Those that call are white and of the same age as I.

White individuals wrote Saginaw history about whites and it was not until the late 1950s or 1960s that black history was introduced into the Saginaw school system. I knew of no black individuals who were recognized by local white authors since I was born in 1923. I am grateful for the friend of Thelma Post who taught all five of the Haithco children in kindergarten at the Fuerbringer School. The friend sent me all the newspaper articles Thelma Post saved regarding me through the years.

I have always been a pack rat and have saved pertinent articles about me that had appeared in the Saginaw (Michigan) News. These articles influenced me to write this autobiography so that our grandparents and grandchildren would be well informed about portions of Saginaw's history.

A lady at the Senior Center in Fayette County, Georgia, where I am currently living, said to me one day, "I told my daughter about you and she said anyone who writes his autobiography is 'self-centered'." Others ask me, "Have you lost your marbles?"

1

Home and Family

A Paradigm Shift
Dad came to Saginaw and married Mom on September 21, 1920. Witnessing the
ceremony were: Elmer B. Warren, Lula Warren and Rev. Peter S. Marks.

From this hour
The summer rose
Sweeter breathes to
Charm us;
From this hour the
Winter snows
Lighter fall to harm us.
Fair or foul—
On land or sea—
Come the wind or weather,
Beast and worse
Whatever they be
We shall share together
Winthrop prayed
(Author unknown)

The Bridal Prayer

They stand alone the newly wed
With chastened voice and reverent head
One flesh the twain and on the prayer
Ascending from the altar there.
Tender and broken is each word
Upon the sacred stillness heard;
Winged with one faith to reach the throne
And bring a Father's blessing down.
Oh! Sweetest hour for human pair,
When love is sanctified by prayer.
And when, in answer from the skies,
God sends again earth's Paradise.
Rankin.

February 7, 1923, I was born in Saginaw, Michigan, to Lady C. Dabney and William J. Haithco. Mother was born in Logansport, Indiana, and my father was born in Paulding, Ohio. My older sister, Lady Margaret, was born a year-and-a-half before me, and through the effect of the theory of evolution, the Darwin theory, and Mother Nature, Dorothy, Montie and Mary Jane were to follow as sisters. If you think raising four sisters is not a problem, just ask me.

Although Margaret and I were born in a little house at 314 S. Seventh Street, we all lived at 2275 Hancock Street, in later years the name changed to Wilson Street and then to Gaylord Street. Our house at 2275 Gaylord Street was on a dead-end street, and the property north of our house belonged to Walter and Sophie Schultz and their twin sons, Lester and Leslie, and Gramma Beyer, Mrs. Schultz's mother from Germany.

This plot ran from Bay Road all the way east to Larry Deno's backyard on Ames Street. We were allowed to take advantage of some of the produce of the garden, which was mostly potatoes.

Our small house was on a 32' by 120' lot. It had been built by Frank Thompson who lived next door with his red head sister Kate. There was a small kitchen, with an adjoining bathroom. There was one step from the kitchen to the outside, with a pump nearby. The living/dining room was about 30' long. The house had two bedrooms, each 12' square, with a closet between—two bedrooms for two parents and five kids! Five kids—four girls and one boy. One sister and I had to sleep in the living room, next to the pot-bellied stove and, on occasion when the fire went out, one of us wet the bed because we did not want to walk to the bathroom on cold floors! We did not ruin the mattress because we slept on a daybed, just wires for a "spring."

The living room was covered with more than one layer of linoleum and then a rug of sorts! The kitchen and bedrooms were covered with linoleum, over a few boards and an old door or two. When the linoleum was worn out one could look through the floor and see the bare ground, as there was no basement under the house. It was just sitting on four round posts.

But we had it good, on $35.00 a week. I know, as I on occasion walked four blocks to Wagar's Drug Store to cash the check. The Atlanta Journal Constitution recently wrote of the life of one Bernie Marcus, co-founder of Home Depot and President of the Marcus Atlanta Aquarium, how he started with his mother making him go to college, and he got his degree in Pharmacy! This is what my Mother did! Hey brother—'Tis not for us to reason why, but 'tis for us to do and die.

Later, Dad built a garage with an area in the back for one ton of soft coal. There was no floor in the garage until later years and Dad poured it himself. We had no car—his bosses had the cars! Dad and Roscoe Johnson dug the water line from the sidewalk to the house. I soon learned that the sewer line and the water line were not the same!

At the northwest corner of the house was a cistern, which is a 200 gallon wooden water tank that would collect and store rain water from the eaves troughs. This was not pure water but it was used for washing clothes, and could be used for bathing if heated and placed in a tub. When I razed the house, there must have been 30 or 40 old marbles in this cistern. In this tank and in Mother's many flowers gardens where many marbles still lay. I had to go to Sunday School and to church, and sing in the choir. I had to join the Cub Scouts.

I had to make sure the coal buckets were full at night. I had to spade the garden next door, 30' x 120' by hand, and then rake the garden. I had to cultivate the garden, pick green beans and strawberries for the Burden Greenhouse, and had to pick gooseberries and currants.

I had to sell magazines, had to take violin lessons, as well as I had to help wash the Packard, LaSalle and the Cadillac at Dad's job. I couldn't drive because we did not have a car.

I did not smoke and I did not know what dope was. I did not belong to any gang. I did not know what a "gang" was. I had to wear knickers until I got into high school, and then I had to press my own slacks. I couldn't have a two-wheel bicycle—it was too dangerous and we did not have any money.

Bernie Marcus contracted with Wolfgang Puck, whose company still operates a catering service at the aquarium!

We all made it in that little two-bedroom bungalow until we completed our schooling. Dad lived and farmed on a farm in Midland, Michigan, amongst four to five other black families. The families included the Browns, Johnsons, Farmers, Randalls, Matthews and probably others whom I have forgotten.

When Dad first moved to Saginaw, he worked for Mr. Walker, who was a painter. Shortly thereafter, Dad became a chauffeur for the John Dwight family. In my early days I looked upon the "position" of chauffeur as a state of servitude. As I grew a little older, I had some dichotomy of my thoughts about this job as I, also, found myself working as a chauffeur to help pay for college.

Many persons have been instrumental in my life and they include The Montagues; S. E. Symons, Sr; Morleys; Win Daileys; R. Perry Shorts; Carl Fletchers; Alex Reids; and I am sure that there were many others whose names I have omitted.

Margaret and I enjoyed going to work with Dad at the big Dwight family home because we had a chance to eat lunch with Dad—bologna and cheese sandwiches on Gramma Beyer's homemade bread with the thick black crust … German-style. When Mr. Dwight died, we received most of his personal effects. There were poker chips, "Put and Take" games, dominoes, PIT game, and of course those large "tubular" ice skates.

I used to stuff facial tissue, stockings or the Saginaw News into the toes of the ice skates in order to make them fit. They were still too wide and my ankles would bow with me "spread-eagle" as I fell. In order to skate at Hoyt Park, we had to walk from Bay and State Streets to Hoyt Park.

Of course, we also loved to ride in a Packard. Shortly after Mr. Dwight died, Dad became a chauffeur for Clifford and Florence Lilley at 1441 Cedar Street. Also during this period, Cronk Street began at Taft Street and proceeded west to Bay Street. Cronk Street began again around Durand Street and progressed east to North Michigan where the name changes to Davenport. Davenport went east to North Washington where it turned into Johnson Street.

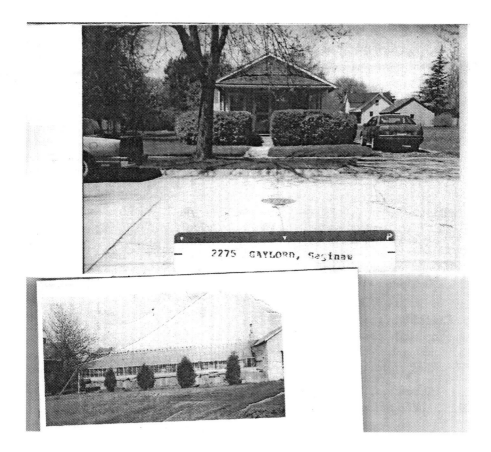

2275 GAYLORD, Saginaw

Attending Fuerbringer was funny in many ways. On the northwest corner of Madison and State Streets lived an elderly man who did small scale farming with two to three horses. We would leave school, walk through his driveway, through his fruit trees, and out to Cronk Street. While walking, we may have collected apples, pears or plums, if he did not see us. We all learned early on that "confiscated" fruits tasted better than fruit that may have been bought in a store. I cannot remember whether or not we went home for lunch, but in mid-morning and mid-afternoon we had graham crackers and milk as a snack at school. Near the corner of Bay and State Streets, was Janson's hamburger stand and next to that was Smitty's barbershop.

The Burden Greenhouses, owned by Will Burden, one of the few black-owned businesses in the county, were also on that street. If memory serves me, the Burdens had about nine children: Harold, Ray, Emerson, Marcus, Russell,

Marie, Mildred, Dorothy, and Lucille. The Burden Greenhouse ran behind the first seven to eight houses west on State Street and then north on Bay to where Frueh's Flower Shop now stands. This area was well represented by fruit trees (apples, pears and plums).

Across the street on Bay, was a Shell gas station owned by Grant Schaeding. Behind the gas station was a long driveway separating the station from the Butlers. Further into the property there were four garages built by Conrad Kundinger for the businesses he built on State Street for the storeowners. We soon found out that Harold Wagar was storing his Shay Water bottles, returned for deposit, in that garage. We would open the door (not break-in) and borrow one. We would then go in the front door of the drugstore, recover our deposit and purchase a popsicle or a bar of candy.

After World War II, we apologized and he said that was okay! The times that I washed his Pontiac Silver Streak or drove to the west side post office to buy stamps for him was considered an "exchange." I wonder if pharmacist Harold Wagar had any influence in my becoming a pharmacist later in life. I told him once about the Texas millionaire who told his son that money was like horse manure. If you spread it around it does a good job. If you leave it in one pile, it simply stinks.

The Schultz Twins and I

Well, now that we have covered the short cut to Cronk Street, let me walk you two blocks to Wilson Street (now Gaylord). It is a long two blocks from Cronk to Morgan. Going north, our house was the last house before the Schultz's garden. The Walter Schultz house was at 2280 Bay Street and the property ran beside our house to the back of the Denno home on Ames (which is now Avon) Street. The Schultz family included Walter and Sophia, twins Lester and Leslie, and Gramma Beyer who came from the old country in 1863. We all lived like people should and could if they simply tried.

When one or more of the children in my family became sick, Gramma Beyer would take the well children over to their house on Bay Road and we would stay there until the sick child became well. The Schultz twins, Lester and Leslie, were raised together with me; we played together and we stayed together. I think Leslie passed away in the late 1970s. Lester and his wife Mary continue to be good friends and it has been over 76 years since this friendship started. We kept our home on Gaylord Street for about 74 years and never complained about a neighbor moving in next door or across the street or down the street. We never had crosses burned in the yard. My mother actually owned five parcels of property on Gaylord Street and sold all of them to Jack Brady, whose mother had the Brady Grocery on the corner of Avon and Morgan. In the late 1940s, Dad thought we would try to build a new home on Gaylord but was told by the lending agency that the "house was too good" for the neighborhood!!!

LESTER SCHULTZ, LESLIE SCHULTZ and BILL HAITHCO in MY 1928 CHEVY

When Lester and Leslie Schultz and I were in our teens, we decided to go hunting in the Midland/Coleman area off US-10. We left the highway and entered the woods somewhere off M-30. Both Schultzes had compasses and 16-gauge shot guns. I had my 20-gauge single shot Savage Shotgun, but couldn't afford a compass. We vacated the car, set our bearing, made rules about getting lost and took off on our own hunting trip. About mid-afternoon, Lester and I crossed the trail Leslie was on and we finally met after climbing a tree and shooting. At dark, we were lost and finally came to a road and started hitchhiking and looking for other people. Soon an old Ford truck came by. The driver asked where we were going and we told him. He said he had seen the car and knew where it was. We got in and he took us right to the car, seven or eight miles from where we started. I do not remember shooting any rabbits.

Farming

We would load the Burden's Ford pickup truck with crates and baskets and drive west on US-10 to Midland, work three to four hours in the gardens and drive back to Saginaw by 8 a.m. to the city market on North Baum Street. For lunch I took the same bologna sandwich I ate at the Dwight home with Dad, only these sandwiches were fresher. This was not the best job in the world, but I learned early that I had to either "cut the mustard" or "lick the jar the mustard came in". I was paid $1.00 a day.

At an early age, when money was low and short, Mother remembered when she was born and raised in Logansport, Indiana they ate dandelion greens cooked with ham. In Saginaw, at 2275 Wilson Street, we would dig these greens in our garden plot and in the long garden plots on the Schultz property. Good soil, as it was tilled every year, few weeds. Dandelion greens must be picked in the early spring when the leaves are young and before the flowers get too big. After the leaves get too big, and the flowers begin to bloom, the dandelions tend to get bitter … maybe good for wine! As I got older, I would walk over to the Deindorfer Woods and dig some greens there. Later I was allowed to go along Shattuck Road, the railroad tracks, where I would pick the greens there and on the periphery of some farmer's property.

As I grew older, I would drive a car over near Aunt Nellie's home, near the Lapeer railroad tracks and 15th Street, where there were, and still are, vacant lots bordering the tracks. This was a good source for greens with little weeds. In 1980, I began my twenty-plus years of fishing in Ontario with Dick Sturm and his Frankenmuth "gang." Whether at Murray Lake or at the 35,000-acre Dog Lake near Missanabie, Ontario, the dandelion greens were large and young, and they grew in the sand, removed from weeds.

The Schultz's truck-farmed all of this property every year and we had the advantage of sharing the produce as well as the chickens (Leghorns and Plymouth Rocks) as well as eggs. Outside of the chicken coop grew some horseradish, which I, on occasion would grind for our use. I think the location of the horseradish roots had something to do with the strength of the finished product. We also had a garden plot beside our house that I had to dig up by hand every spring in order to plant the garden. We mainly grew potatoes, green beans, lettuce, corn, onions, radishes, carrots, green peas, lima beans, cabbage, pickles, jalapeno peppers, red beets and green peppers. While working in our "truck farm" garden, some items needed special care in planting.

The cucumber pickles needed to be planted in a 3.1416-inch mound and little did I know, as I planted these cucumber seeds, that in 2003 I would read an ad in the Avon® book of their products about "cucumber melon" cosmetics.

WOW—would I have become rich?? Lately I also walked down the ointment/creams section of a local grocery store and I saw a product called "Capsaicin Cream". Capsaicin is the substance in the jalapeno pepper that makes it hot. The cream is used for topical pain. Boy, did I miss the boat!! Oh, well, I guess I missed a lot.

We would be in Ontario fishing for seven days, and on the night before we broke camp I would go out with my paring knife and a large garbage bag and dig a full bag of dandelion greens. Yes, I would have to clean them when I got home but at that age a bottle of beer would be added and the work would be easier to complete. About the last two or three years, when we were in Canada, I noticed some "fiddleheads" at the fresh produce counter, so Frankenmuthers were treated with a meal of a New England delicacy—fiddleheads! If you ever wander to Ontario, stop in, off Highway 651 and north of Highway 101.

Bill Stroup

Magazine Sales

About this time I also began selling magazines, Colliers and Woman's Home Companion. My "route" took me about nine miles. I mostly walked the route and this took me all day. One magazine was weekly and the other was published monthly. When the monthly magazine came out, Mom very often went with me to help. I would go from State and Bay Streets east to Holland and Fourth Streets, north to Fourteenth and Janes Streets, north to Dr. Sumby's office on Farwell and Fifth Streets, to the County Infirmary (now the location of the Veterans Administration Hospital), then home with many stops in-between. The awards I received for sales—I used to get glass dinnerware for Mom!

As my magazine business increased, I found the business required more time and energy. I needed a little more time to service the additional customers and to arrive home before dark. It was a rule that we could not have a bicycle for two reasons: they were too expensive and they were dangerous. Two houses east of the corner of Gaylord and Cronk Streets lived the Clayton family. They had three children, Marshall, Ollie and a daughter. I made a "deal" with Marshall to rent his bike for fifty cents a day to deliver my magazines. The very first time I rented the bike, I was on my way home crossing Genesee at the bridge, going down the decline at the Doyle hamburger stand, and I heard a "beep, beep". I looked to my left and the beep came from my father's car, with motions for me to "pull over," which I immediately did. Dad stopped the car, got out, opened the trunk, placed the bike in the trunk, opened his hand and spanked me. Then we drove home. We made the first stop at the Clayton's home to drop off the bike. Our house was the last one on the street (blocked by the Schultz's garden and a dead-end). It was time for my engagement with Dad's hand and I couldn't go anywhere.

Music

About 1930, I began taking violin lessons from J. P. Davidson at the corner of South Washington and Hayden Streets, in the Germain Building. The first floor of this building was the Germain Piano Company; the second floor was the Edwina Wright Dance Studio; and the fourth floor housed the Davidson violin lesson area. Mr. Davidson also made violins in this area. Mr. Davidson was very strict. He made me count and cry simultaneously as I played and he pounded on the music stand with his violin bow! I continued my violin lessons until the tenth grade when Mr. Davidson died, and I would not take lessons from his brother who came to Saginaw from Canada to teach violin. At this time, I became acquainted with the open market when Mr. Burden asked me to work for him on his greenhouse/garden. He had property in Midland County at Mt. Haley Township where he grew green beans, radishes, strawberries, etc.

The Bowmans

My friend and playmate, Charles Bowman, lived on South Seventh Street, on the other side of town near the Women's Hospital, and across the street from Jackie Marxhausen and around the corner from Chuckie and Leonard Malotte's house.

I could ride the bus across town, get off at Seventh and Janes Streets, walk three doors and play with Chuck's electric train, steam shovel, marbles, baseball cards, and even ride his bike.

Another good thing about my friendship with Charles Bowman—his mother Nancy was from Canada and every summer his father would take me along with the Bowmans to London, Ontario, Canada for vacation. We stayed at Charles' Aunt Alice's home and visited the Penny Park where we could play in the wading pool, ride horses, or spend our money in the Penny Arcade. Charles was very fortunate as his father and Charles DeGroat were the only black employees for many years at Michigan Bell Telephone Company in Saginaw. Also in those days, many automobile companies changed their product style every year. Mr. Bowman bought a new Ford every year and Charles got a new watch every year. So when we went to Ontario in the summers, Charles would loose his watch. Mr. Bowman would buy him a new watch Every Year.

The Lilley Family

Again, having Dad work in "servitude" required an attitude adjustment—we had some money, our clothing, food and family, but NO BIKE! The Lilley family were members of the "400 set" and parties were common. The main annual affair was the Charity Ball, held at the Bancroft Hotel. Dad worked day and night on this event and we benefited by getting the leftovers. This might include turkey, open-faced sandwiches of caviar, egg salad, seafood, anchovies (WOW), shrimp cocktail and an assortment of cheeses. We received similar favors at Thanksgiving and Christmas (but no bike). Mr. Lilley was president of the Vogt Manufacturing Company on Lycaste Avenue, in Detroit, Michigan. Every Monday, Dad would drive Mr. Lilley to Detroit's Statler Hotel and return on Fridays to bring him back to Saginaw.

How well I remember working at the YMCA on North Michigan and the Ames Street Methodist church when they had dinner meetings for service clubs and such groups. The women's groups prepared the meals and I served them. Freshly prepared food, no powdered mashed potatoes, and I got all I could eat. By the time I walked home at the end of the day, I wasn't hungry … still I had no bike.

During the summers, the Lilley's would go to their summer home in East Tawas, at the Tawas Beach Association. Bill Stonehouse was the caretaker of this beautiful five-bedroom cottage on Lake Huron.

I think Joe and Ann Mason (the Lilleys' niece) still own the cottage. The Masons were in the paint business and lived in Grosse Pointe Farms, Michigan. The Lilley cottage had a three-car garage with a second floor, screened-in porch, landscaped yards and mahogany motorboat, either a Gar Wood or Chris Craft, with a large Lycoming inboard engine. Across from the cottage was a small one-room cabin where Dad stayed. In later years, after finishing college, we would go to Dad's cabin for smelt dipping around Easter when the smelt were running.

The creek in Tawas starts out on the beach, two inches deep, meanders through the Moulthrop property up through the trees, through the drain tile, under the road and on to the Coast Guard road. I remember the time that Dad, Harry Weaver (chauffer of the George Morgans from Frankenmuth, Michigan), and I drove to East Tawas, leaving Saginaw about midnight. The smelt started running about 2:30 a.m. and in about an hour, we had our little water pail full. So we opened the big garage, found a 55-gallon wooden barrel, rolled it down to the car and filled it with more smelt. Just before daybreak, the run was still going so we went back to the garage, got an old metal upright ice container and filled it up and finally we retrieved an old, chipmunk-eaten awning from the garage and also filled this with smelt. We put all of this in the open spaces in the trunk of my Buick convertible. As we crossed the railroad tracks south of Standish, the rear bumper guard hit the pavement, but there was no damage … but my kingdom for a bike.

As we arrived back in Saginaw, we began giving the smelt away about 9 a.m. People came out of their homes with one quart plastic bowls. Our last stop was at Kent Drug Store where Ralph Kent and his father came out with a plastic bucket and said, "Take the rest of the barrel out to my home on Kind Road and spread the smelt over my front yard for fertilizer." The next time I go smelt dipping at East Tawas, I will take two-pound postal priority mail boxes, and send the smelt to my friends with the message "I will Bill you"!

Sometimes my Dad would have to work on Sundays and I would go with him. Mr. Lilley would send me to Gray's Drug store at Holland and Sheridan for the Sunday newspaper for which I was paid fifty cents. Across the street from the Lilley's at 1432 Cedar was the Samuel E. Symons family where I eventually became the recipient of a Saturday "job". On Saturday at 8 a.m. I would go to work with Dad and go across the street to the Symons' house, wash and simonize the Buick, cut the grass, rake the lawn, stoke the furnace, wash the basement floor and steps and, on occasion, make up the beds. Sometimes, I would have to drive Marion Eddy Symons on a few errands. When Sam Jr. finished Northwestern

University, I catered the dinner and also catered the reception when he married the daughter of Al Riedel.

For working on Saturdays I was paid $1.00—that was for the entire day. But as I had mentioned earlier, I knew I had to cut the mustard or lick the jar the mustard came in. Now I can remember when I owned my own pharmacy and belonged to the Chamber of Commerce, we had a summer job program for college students, and I would tell the students that we had telephone calls requesting help cutting grass in Lathrup Park. The students would typically answer, "Well, I am in college to become a doctor or a lawyer … I cannot cut grass". To this I would respond, "Well, come back when you have your shingle".

Win Dailey

Winthrop Dailey was owner of the Dailey Pickle Company and a friend of the Symons. One winter he asked me to accompany him, his son Jim, Bill Standish of the Hammond Standish Meat Packing Company of Detroit, Michigan, and an oil man from Mount Pleasant, Michigan, to Dailey cottage on the Au Sable River for deer hunting.

I drove one of the cars, cooked the meals, and was the bartender as well as the person who kept the fire in the fireplace. As I recall, we left Saginaw on Thanksgiving Day, and by Sunday, no deer had been shot. Bill Standish said he thought he would go back to Detroit, check on his business and return on Monday evening. Eventually all decided to return home and come back Monday. I said I would stay in camp and watch the cottage and the expensive rifles. They told me there was a small lodge for women about seven miles away … what would I do there? They left and I was there without any car so I would go to bed at sundown and get up at sunup. I found where two deer trails were located, crossing approximately 100 yards behind the cabin. I would eat breakfast, get my folding chair and rifle and walk to the crossing. I would sit there until the sun was at its zenith, go in for lunch and then go back out to the crossing until sundown. At dinnertime, I would return to the cottage, fix the fire and get in bed in the front room. I would lie there, listening to the constant ripple of the Au Sable until I fell asleep. Monday night about 10:30 p.m. there was a break in the cadence, which sounded like something walking up the log steps from the direction of the river to the front of the cottage. Then the sounds came from around the cottage so I got up, went outside and onto the back porch and there was a large buck deer slowly walking back into the woods. Question—should I shoot him? I have no license to hunt!!! No. No. By noon on Monday, no one had come back to the cottage and I had some eerie feelings. About 3:15 p.m. I saw the headlights of a Cadillac Coupe coming down the hill toward the cottage.

I went to the back porch to greet Jim Dailey and when he opened the car door, I said "Hi, Jim," and my own voiced scared the stuffing out of me. Recently I read the book, "The Grizzly Years" by Doug Peacock. Doug had enlisted in the Green Berets in World War II, and he spoke of the times he was on surveillance for three or four days in Vietnam and never saw or talked to anyone. He spoke frankly about the effect this had on him. How well I can relate to this story after my days alone in the cottage.

Parable of the Pebbles

I can never properly thank my parents, Lady C. and William J. Haithco, for buying our little home on Hancock Street in 1923. We had to attend the public schools located in our school district and I am grateful that these schools taught me to say such things as:

"I should have been there" rather than "I ought to been there"

"I don't have any money" rather than "I aint got no money"

"Send the money to me" rather than "Send the money to myself"

"Where is the First State Bank?" rather than "Where is the First State Bank at?"

"All you people should read this book" rather than "All yuz should read dis book" or "I ate all of my dinner" rather than "I et all my dinner"

When I turn on the television today, it is disgusting to hear all the grammar, sentence structure, and verbiage that are being used. Are some of our teachers teaching incorrectly or are the parents to blame? I can recall the "Parable of the Pebbles" that tells of a gentleman walking along the beach one evening and as he walked in the moonlight his feet became a little sore. When he complained, a voice said, "Bend thou over and gather a few stones." The next morning when he awakened there among the stones was a diamond, one emerald and one ruby.

And like education, he was glad he had collected some of the stones along the way but sorry that he had not gathered more.

Discoverer Motor Home

In April 1971, I decided to purchase a motor home, the Discoverer-25 from the Cadillac dealer in Flint, Michigan. This was the 25-foot motor home designed by Seman "Bunkey" Knudsen who started his factory in Brighton, Michigan. At this point in my life, I was being pressed in my business by the construction of I-675, the bypass of I-75 around Saginaw. I had had my pharmacy for about 14 years and was contemplating working for Saginaw General Hospital as staff pharmacist. My "excuse" for the purchase was my son Jai's 10th birthday, but naturally it was for the use by all the family as I had had only six days of vacation during my business ownership, and I thought now I would be able to take planned vacations with my family.

I left the motor home at the dealership in Flint as I was somewhat "afraid" of that 25-foot vehicle. I would go to Flint on a number of occasions and drive the vehicle around the parking lot and re-park it and return to Saginaw. After a couple of weeks, my friend Jack Wesseley, who worked in the circulation department of the Saginaw News, stopped by my pharmacy and said, "When are you going to get that motor home? We have to go to Black Lake on a fishing trip with our boys." So in a week, Jack stopped by early in the morning and he drove me to Flint to pick up my new motor home. It was long, it was wide, and it had all my pride! I made all the curves and parked it in our driveway. When my wife first saw it she said, "I am not going to ride in that thing." So there goes the pin in my balloon!

And it was Billy, Shari, Jai, and I who enjoyed the motor home. We went to picnics, family reunions in Lima, Ohio, football games, and general sight seeing trips with our cousins Muggs and Bernetta of Lima, Ohio. The motor home stayed in my possession until July 1992, when I sold it, as the storage and maintenance was a problem and all my children were grown. This ownership was an experience, as the motor home was very "eye-catching" with its aerodynamic design.

2

School Days

Fuerbringer School

All five of us kids went to Fuerbringer School, which at that time was located at the corner of Madison and State Streets; this corner is now home to the Salvation Army. Madison Street is also now named North Carolina Street. I remember the school had about six rooms: the principal's office and kindergarten through fourth grades. Shortly after Margaret and I finished the second grade, I think the new Fuerbringer School on Madison (Carolina) Street was built and this is the site to this date. While it was being built, I had to attend Stone School and Margaret attended Herig. My kindergarten teacher, Thelma Post, taught me the other uses of a 12-inch ruler other than for measuring. It was at Fuerbringer that I recited my first poem. I do not remember the author of this poem but it was recited in Miss Eleanor Burnside's class.

Eldorado
Gaily bedight
A gallant Knight
In sunshine and in shadow
Hard journeyed long
Singing his song
In search of Eldorado.
But he grew old
This Knight so bold
And o'er his heart fell a shadow
Before he found
A spot of ground
That looked like Eldorado
(Author Unknown)

Miss Burnside came to Saginaw from Rockford, Illinois, and was my fourth grade teacher. I also had her again for my sixth grade teacher. She always was my favorite teacher.

She had a kiss for me inside of the classroom. Outside of the classroom, she always gave me recognition, even when I waited at the downtown Cunningham's drugstore for the State Street bus to take me home from my violin lesson. Miss Burnside was Swedish and she taught us how to yodel ... "Hansel and Gretel, lived down in the valley ... Ouee ah ah, ouee ah ..." What our country needs is more kisses and fewer bullets!

I was compelled to wear knickers to school and all social events because Mom said I was too big for my britches. If I must wear knickers rather than long pants, then I must wear wool anklets and knee socks to be "sharp" as I thought. Later, Mr. Lilley was known to wear French Shriner and Urner shoes. I would get the shoes as "hand-me-downs" and if I could find enough cotton or facial tissue, I would stuff this into the toes of the shoes to make them fit. I was rather "sharp" from the knees downward!! And, who cares, I was afraid to dance at the dances anyway.

Going to Fuerbringer was fun in many ways. Once a month, they had a PTA meeting and children were allowed to attend; they may have been a part of the program. Oh, how well I remember the Young family (parents of Buddy and Betty Ann), the Hanley family (parents of Jim and Lawrence), the Ahrens family (parents of Dorothy and Eleanor), the Voelkers (parents of Lois and Aldean), the Wolbers (parents of Ann and Ralph), the Messengers (parents of Bob), the Rushlows (I have forgotten the children's names), the Schultzes (parents of Lester and Leslie), the Butzins (parents of Gerry), the Ochmans (parents of Johnny), the Jahns (parents of Bob), the Vaseys (parents of Ruth), the Vetengels (parents of Ruth), the Kitzmans (parents of Art), the Tompkins (parents of Mildred), the Stuedmanns (parents of Gene and Howard), the Schieswohls (parents of Erna), the Claytons (parents of Lyle) and many other parents whose names I have now forgotten.

North Intermediate School

From the sixth to the ninth grade, I attended North Intermediate School. We had to change classrooms almost every hour with different teachers in each room. My first educational venue ... our first big test in conformity and organization. I also had to plan for lunch. One could go home if time allowed or one could bring brown bag lunches. Mine often contained ham salad sandwiches, egg salad sandwiches, bologna sandwiches, boiled eggs, fruit or whatever Mom had time and money to prepare. Then we ate our meal in either the girls' or boys' gym where you mixed with the bouquet of gym shoes, boiled eggs, onions, orange peels or maybe French onion soup. Those who had the money might go outside and buy a hot dog, cotton candy, popcorn, or a greasy hamburger … greasy but good! Perhaps a candied apple was purchased for dessert. There were five blacks at North Intermediate School—Jack and Cleo Nash, Evelyn Burden and Margaret and Bill Haithco.

Sometimes, if Dad had time, he would come to school and pick us up for lunch then get us back by 1 p.m. The Lilley family lived at 1441 Cedar Street, corner of Holland, so it was a quick, direct shot to and from North Intermediate School. Our peers really enjoyed seeing us get out of a Cadillac one day, a LaSalle another day and a Packard another day. Ray Heagany (Heagany and Draper Chevrolet) lived across from the Lilley's and every year when the new Chevrolets came out, Clifford Lilley bought Mr. Heagany's "old Chevy" and gave it to Dad. We still came out in pretty good shape.

North Intermediate School was a change in schooling with intramural sports, lunches, band, and orchestra. I continued taking my private violin lessons and became the North Intermediate Orchestra Concert Master. As such, I was leader of the first violin section; I played solo selections and at times served as assistant conductor. Earl Summerville, our band/orchestra leader, was the one who sold me my E-flat alto saxophone. I think I wanted to become a "Johnny Hodges" like the one in Duke Ellington's orchestra. Mr. Summerville taught me how to play the scales and that's the last I remember. No one ever told me that the quickest way to Carnegie Hall was practice, practice, practice.

Arthur Hill High School

Now comes the fall of 1937, and on the southwest corner of Court and Harrison stands the Arthur Hill High School where I matriculated for three years. The school with external, spiral, metal fire escape tunnels. The school with the annex on the second floor that had speed bumps on the floor. The Butman Fish Library with Miss Oppenheim, Hinds and Weinbergs Drug Store with cherry cokes, banana milkshakes, tin roof vanilla milkshakes with butter pecan ice cream and other commonly prescribed items. On the street on Michigan Avenue was the YMCA where Charlie Crittenden and Harvey Spaulding waited to serve you the "Y" way. Who can't venture to speak of the old Arthur Hill High School without mentioning the erudite Irl Brock and Ray Morrow, stately and always in control.

One of the students, J. Spencer Kelly, had a somewhat controlling manner. I turned around one day and Spence was standing on the steps on Court Street campaigning. Who for? Bill Haithco for Student Council. Spence and I were not in the same class but after this event (which I won), he and I became very close friends. I had two sport coats and Spence had two sport coats. Spence lived on Hamilton Street above Bauer and Bauer's Cleaners with his mother and stepfather, Mr. and Mrs. Carl Bauer. Prior to our "tea dances", Spence and I would go to his house and swap sport coats for the social event. Later in life, I would name my youngest son Jai Spencer Haithco, after Spence.

June 1934.

William H. Haithco
Class of 1940

-PROGRAM-

PRESIDING	Mr. Thomas S. Sharpe
PRELUDE	Arthur Hill Band
	Mr. Timothy Kaznia, Director
PATRIOTIC CEREMONY	Audience
ARTHUR HILL VOCAL ENSEMBLE	Mr. Donald Fittje, Director
STUDENT CHAIRPERSON	Tayduen Mustapha
HONOR ALUMNUS TRIBUTE AND PRESENTATION	Anna Glass
RESPONSE	Mr. William Haithco
INDUCTION OF NATIONAL HONOR SOCIETY MEMBERS	Michael Dennison
	1991 National Honor Society President
	Evan Pritchett
	1991 National Honor Society Vice-President
ALMA MATER	Arthur Hill Vocal Ensemble and Audience

Oh, Arthur Hill, our love for you
Forever will be staunch and true.
We love your ivy-covered walls
The laughter of your spacious halls
With loyal hearts and voices raise
And with devotion sing your praise
Oh, Alma Mater, hearts to you
And memories of the Gold and Blue.

RECEPTION

PLATFORM GUESTS

Mr. Robert Dennis, President of the Board of Education
Dr. Foster B. Gibbs, Superintendent

An article in the Saginaw News highlighted the Honor Alumnus award from Arthur Hill High School in 1991. The article summarized my civic achievements in Saginaw County.

Certificate of

Appreciation

May it be known by all who read this that this Certificate of Appreciation has been presented to

William H. Haithco

For

Enthusiastic Support

Presented this 24th *Day of* June *, 19*91

ARTHUR HILL HIGH SCHOOL

My older sister, Margaret, was a year and a half older than I and she graduated from Arthur Hill High School in 1939. She enrolled at Bay City Junior college, awakening to the fact that getting back and forth to Bay City (Michigan) was a task. One had to learn how to bum a ride with some other students, if possible! In 1940, Dad bought a car. He had a friend, Ruben Burke, also a chauffeur, who lived in a big house across from Provanzano's Grocery on West Genesee. In the garage was a 1928 Chevrolet two-door sedan that had been setting on wooden blocks for years. It had original white "cord" tires and 18,000 miles on the odometer. The brakes were the "band-type"—on the back wheels, which were made of wooden spokes, were bands. One would place a crescent wrench through the spokes and tighten or loosen the bands to adjust the brakes. This adjusting process turned out to be needed almost everyday and sometimes in the middle of a trip depending on the humidity. But at $50.00, what a bargain. My Mom came up with the money to buy this car (she owned Consumer's Power stock probably before the time of Einstein). About once a month, Margaret and I would go to Seitner's and buy a different pattern of cloth and make new seat covers for our very high profile Chevy.

The new Arthur Hill High School was dedicated in January, 1940, and I was the host since I was on the student council. About mid-afternoon, Mr. and Mrs. Robert Leckie came to my station on the second floor near the little theater and asked if I would please drop their daughter Barbara at home in the Golfside area when the ceremonies were completed. Sure! It rained practically all day and I had half of the rain on the front passenger seat—the window was broken vertically. I felt bad that I had no window until I met a man who had no car.

I graduated from Arthur Hill in 1940 and enrolled in Bay City Junior college also, majoring in mathematics. Shortly thereafter, a relative of Uncle Joe Ely died in St Louis, Michigan, and left a 1937/38 Packard 120 to Dad for us kids to use. This was great until I went to a football game in Ann Arbor, Michigan, in the fall of 1940 and my anti-freeze boiled over in all of the football traffic. The car caught fire so I called Dad to ask what I should do. He said fill the radiator with water and drive the car home. I just couldn't wait for my lecture.

3

Military Service

World War II

During my second year in Junior College, Saginaw postmaster John Mershon told my Dad there were applications in his office for examinations for position of War Ordnance Inspector. This was the first part of World War II and the draft was threatening me so I took the Civil Service examination and passed. I was sent to the University of Michigan for a three-month training program in the School of Engineering. I was the first black student to live in the Law Quadrangle but I was not a law student. It then seemed that the government had an affinity for law students and they were drafted very quickly. My specialized training in the School of Engineering consisted of blueprint writing and reading, use of measuring devices, surface gauges, micrometers, calipers, hardness testing, tensile strength and all ancillary attitudes and activities. I completed the course with flying colors and was sent to the Saginaw Steering Gear Plant #2, the gun plant, to be a government inspector. General Motors had their own inspectors and the United States Government had their own inspectors. The specifications of the General Motors Corporation were less stringent than those of the U.S. Government. If 10% of the lot the government inspected were not within allowable tolerances, we would deny for government purchase. The parts we inspected were triggers, breach locks, barrels, firing pins, bullet casings, and all other component parts for the carbine and Sub-machine guns. General Motors had a female inspector in the inspection department. She was from Rock, Michigan, and over a short time she became very friendly. Notes on inspection sheets were passed through the dividing "fence" and we became very good friends. I had no car so we would meet some mornings at a restaurant.

Occasionally in the summer when I was living with the Montagues, I would have Bob Montague's car and we might go for a ride in the evening. Sometimes we would just hire a taxi and we would ride to Bay City and back. I think it is time for a paradigm shift about now. I should have changed the way I did things.

I began saving for a car and I soon moved to Mrs. Brown's home on South Fourth, near Holland. It wasn't long before the government made the paradigm shift for me. I was inducted into the Army. Yes, I still needed that bike but that wasn't too practical now.

Me and the armeeeeeeeeeeeeeeeeeeeee. I was inducted at Fort Custer, Battle Creek, Michigan, and was soon sent to Sheppard Field, in Wichita Falls, Texas, in the Air Force. After some more basic training, a few bottles of scotch, a few scrapes with the rednecks of Wichita Falls and Fort Still, Oklahoma, expunging a few "whites only" signs in public places, I received orders to go to Camp Crowder, Missouri, on Detached Service in the communications school. Camp Crowder was a communications school for all armed services and located near the little town of Neosho, Missouri, a town of about 1,300 people. The next large town was Joplin, Missouri, with a population of 40,000 people. Yes, both towns were small but both had their offerings.

Neosho was, I believe, about nine miles from camp and the "bus station" was a semi-abandoned gas station. (I was at the age now where I could hardly use that bike!) It wasn't long before we found out there was a place in town near the gas station where one could buy liquor on Sunday. This was behind the Pink Elephant Restaurant. Behind this restaurant was a tall set of steps leading up the back wall to an apartment where a lady and her daughter lived. We climbed the fifteen to twenty steps ending at the apartment door. I was the first in line. The lady came to the window after I knocked and asked what we wanted. I answered nervously "whiskey".

She proceeded to open the door and we walked into the kitchen area where we were seated at a large, center-posted table. I asked how much and she responded "$2.00 per pint". We all concurred, and I noticed her fumbling around in the hallway, moving shoes, boots, slippers and galoshes around, looking for an empty bottle. I heard her ask her daughter if she had a bottle in her room to which the daughter answered "yes".

A clear bottle was finally found and the process was completed. The marketing package was set on the table in front of me and I noticed something in the bottom of the bottle that had the appearance of "mother"—that thick, stringy, bummy, slimy substance that collects in vinegar sometimes. Wanting to rectify the situation, I picked up the bottle and made a close inspection. The "thing" in the bottle was an embryonic mouse!!! We called this to her attention and she yelled. We then decided if she could get a new bottle, break the seal in our presence and fill it with whiskey, we would then complete our purchase. So she obtained a clean water glass, placed it into the corner of her cast-iron sink and emptied the contaminated whiskey into the glass as if she were destroying the whiskey. She then got a clean pint bottle and filled it up with "clean whiskey" (Three Feathers) and we were through. I am certain that the next customer for the day received the whiskey with that nasty, ratty, vermin which was extra flavoring for someone else who wanted to purchase some whiskey. Was this Neosho whiskey or No-show whiskey?

Once we got to Joplin a Mr. Dial, a school principal who had befriended four or five of us GIs, would take us to Coffeyville where there was a college with a shortage of males. We would stay at the home of a couple that owned a restaurant there. This couple was a little older than we were and they were very amenable to parties as was Mr. Dial. Often times when we were partying, they would send food to us from the restaurant at meal times.

Citizens like this could be found in most of the larger cities near Armed Forces Facilities. Joplin was about 40 miles from Neosho and there was a service club located there. We went to Joplin often. I was originally supposed to go to Camp Crowder on detached service to communications school for about three months training. But after my training period was over, I received my Skilled Teletype Installer-Repairman Certificate and I remained there for about eleven months as an instructor. Then one day the mail sergeant walked by across the concourse and he hollered, "Hey, Daniel Field, Georgia". I met him later at the office and he told me he had orders for me to leave for Daniel Field. The information that I had received during my younger years about Georgia was that this was not a place for me. So I went to headquarters and was relieved of this trip. My visit to headquarters also indicated that I was supposed to be stationed in the ASTP training program in Laramie, Wyoming, the entire time that I spent at Camp Crowder. I have yet to see Laramie.

Shortly thereafter, I received my orders to transfer to Maxwell Field in Montgomery, Alabama, to continue my Air Force career. Some days a compatriot and I would be put in a GI truck and taken to Montgomery to work in a civilian business, repairing typewriters. All that I remember is the business was being run by a man named Basil who serviced the base typewriters and we were not paid for our service above our army pay. But it was a new venue and it was fun working "off base". We still had to adhere to our armed forces customs and protocols and it was not long before I again received orders to move. This time … Daniel Field, Georgia!!! There was no room for deliberation and I decided that I had better follow orders and go. This actually turned out to be a little base near Mariana, Florida. I settled in and it wasn't long before one of the soldiers from Chicago, Illinois, said to me, "Why don't you go into town and party?"

Being a little shy about being in the south, I stayed on base, played pool and occasionally found a blackjack card game and also learned how to play chess. One morning I awoke and at the foot of my bunk was a watermelon. When I cut it, the center "meat" was dark yellow and I was so shocked. I thought that someone had played some kind of trick on me and that the melon was not ripe. But my friend from Chicago, whom I called "the city slicker," said it was a sugar melon and I ate it…. it was very good!

The next weekend, Carlton, the city slicker from Chicago, invited me to go into town with him since he wanted me to meet some of his friends. I accepted and we went to Mariana to a "house" at the edge of town, knocked on the door and a lady welcomed us. As we sat in the living room, I noticed cracks in the floor and I heard chickens cackling. I looked through the cracks and saw bare ground. Then an occassional pig. The lady I was supposed to meet was taking a bath in the bathroom. The tub was a large galvanized tub that all members of the family used to bathe after boiling water on the stove. This, to me was hard to take, but this was also Mariana, Florida. I can look back and remember taking baths in a galvanized tub. Three days later, four of us were riding into town in a weapons carrier and we passed this farm and in the middle of a watermelon patch stood Carlton with a hoe in his hands, cultivating melons.

I did not go into town much after these venues and shortly thereafter I received orders to transfer to Goodman Field, Kentucky, with Colonel Benjamin O. Davis' 477th Composite Group, 602nd Air Engineering Squadron, located just outside Fort Knox. It was there that I received training for overseas activities. I liked this assignment—we were near Detroit, Michigan, and Louisville, Kentucky, and a three-day pass wasn't hard to get. I would get a carton of Lucky Strike cigarettes for Walter Schultz and a carton of Chesterfield cigarettes for Harlan Haas and come home to visit my family and the Rev. Charles A. Hill family in Detroit, Michigan. I often roomed for free at 1660 W. Grand Boulevard in Detroit. It was the Haithco habit to stay with friends and family whenever possible as the rent was cheaper and the food was much better.

On one of my visits home, I was in Wagar's drugstore and the Dietzel girl who was a clerk asked when I was returning to Goodman Field. I gave her the date and she, her husband and their 2-year-old son invited me to ride back to Fort Knox with them. It was a nice tight ride in a little coupe until we got into Kentucky when they asked me to take their son to the restroom. We were stopped at once and I was told that I couldn't do that … we weren't the same color. We were all devastated to say the least. Time for another paradigm shift? Change the way that we do things.

Getting Ready for Separation

Shortly after our return, we were processed and sent to Freeman Field, Seymour, Indiana, to prepare for discharge. This was 1946. When I returned home, I resumed my part-time jobs at the Saginaw Club and the Saginaw Country Club. One evening at a club dinner party, I walked past the billiard room and Bob Montague, Sr. playing billiards. He asked me what I was doing and I told him nothing. I had applied to the University of Michigan College of Pharmacy and was told that the school was "filled." I lived a number of summers in the Montague residence, the home of the Robert S. Montague, Sr., family at 1581 S. Washington before entering the service. Bob Montague was the owner of the Saginaw Sugar Beet Products Company on S. Lyons Street. They made SBS-11 and SBS-15, if my memory serves me correctly; they were soaps used commercially for washing hands, etc. There appeared in a local newspaper some time ago that there was no sugar beet substance in the soap.

One of my jobs with the Montagues was taking Mr. Montague to work some mornings and one morning he decided to show me the company. He told me the SBS products were simply the soap "Palmolive beads," to which they added dried sugar beet skins that had been ground to different degrees of coarseness to provide the GRIT! Perhaps we ALL can provide some HISTORY!

At the Montagues', I was chauffeur, cook, bartender … you name it. In a couple of weeks, he called and told me that I had been admitted to the College of Pharmacy. Bob had a relative, Bert Watkins, who was Provost there and he made all of my proper arrangements.

4

Higher Education

Michigan State University
College and Greek Life

In 1948, brothers of Alpha Phi Alpha fraternity founded the Gamma Tau Chapter at Michigan State University. I was one of the founders of that chapter and a charter member. Oh me, this was quite an honor.

The founders of Gamma Tau were motivated by a desire for brotherhood, friendship, welfare, companionship, and a spirit of high idealism. It was also a desire to create an environment that would help others in the years to come. This desire to help has lasted throughout the years. "What a man does for himself will die with him. What he does for others will live forever."

Following is the speech I gave at the Founder's Day meeting:

It is a pleasure meeting here with you tonight on this Founders' Day occasion, and I bring greetings from the founders, all wishing you great wealth, health, and success.

From Bro. Burnett this word: "A learned fool is one who has read everything and simply remembered it."

From Bro. Thompson: "Most men are like eggs; too full of themselves to hold anything else."

From Bro. Johnson: "Live within your income, even though you have to borrow to do so."

From Bro. Richard Caliman: "Life is short, but it is long enough to ruin any man who wants to be ruined."

From Bro. Armstrong: "A man with a small head is like a pin without any; very apt to get into things beyond his depth."

From Bro. Sharp: "It is pretty hard to tell what does bring happiness; poverty and wealth have both failed."

From Bro. Haithco: "There is one advantage of being poor; a doctor will cure you faster."

In parting, this poem to you, Brothers of Gamma Tau:

Man may break his bondage.

Man may break the law.

But there is not a man who is strong enough

To break the bond of Gamma Tau.

Bro. Haithco

I graduated from Michigan State University in 1950 with a degree in Physiology and Pharmacology.

Bill, the "G" Man

After my first year at Michigan, I had to move to Lansing, Michigan, where two of my sisters, Margaret and Dorothy, lived. The cost of living was much less there and I had jobs working for pay. I worked at the Capital on the top floor in the driver's license bureau sorting applications. I often worked from 4 p.m. until midnight. On weekends, I worked as bartender at the Lansing Country Club. In the summer when school was not in session, I worked for the City of Lansing picking up garbage. In the summer months, I learned that garbage was picked up twice as often as in other months so a second crew was necessary. The second crew mainly consisted of graduate students, football players and others who needed jobs and money.

I will never forget my first day when the big steel bedded truck came to the top of the hill at Saginaw and Washington Avenues. The truck came to a stop, the driver got out and started yelling, "Take four and bring four back". This meant take four clean, 20-pound cans and go behind the row houses and pick up four filled cans of garbage and bring all four out to Washington Avenue at the curb. One had to learn how to take it: the weight of the 20-pound steel cans and the humor from the 200-pound pickers. One picker would say, "When you get off work, go home and take a nice cold shower." The next one might throw what you thought was a handful of rice pudding but was, perhaps, a handful of maggots. With a proper mind set, it was rather nice living in Lansing with the academia setting and making enough money to eat, go to school, socialize and save for that return to the University of Michigan.

University of Michigan

I returned to Ann Arbor in the fall of 1950 to complete my pharmacy program. With a new life, I had a job in the Alpha Delta House where I worked for my meals and a job at Witham's Pharmacy on South University Avenue for spending money. My last term in school I had a bank account with a balance of $2.12 and I still had to purchase some pencils for school!

My last two years in college were enjoyable since I wasn't worrying about how I would get my next dollar. During the last two or three weeks of classes, our class president asked me how to get to Midland (Michigan) and I gave him directions (and we did not have Interstate 75). He had noticed an announcement on the bulletin board saying there was an opening in a Midland pharmacy for a pharmacist. When Fred Germer came back to Ann Arbor he said, "Billy, Community Drugs needs three more pharmacists. Why don't you apply?" I took his suggestion and wrote my letter, and soon the answer returned ... "Thank you for inquiring, but I think you might have a problem finding a place to stay in Midland." I wasn't looking for a place to stay in Midland. I was looking for a job. I could have driven a Moped or rode a bike from my house in Saginaw to work. But, oh, well, wrong color again. Thanks, Fred, for the recommendation. Time for a paradigm shift. We should change the way we do things.

5

The Pharmacist

The Pharmacist

Before my official graduation, an attorney from Saginaw called me and said that a friend of his in Saginaw, a pharmacist, had talked to him about his desire to get a black pharmacist in his business. He sounded very concerned and said he wanted to plan for his retirement, that the job would be for approximately one year without any profit sharing and that during the second year there would be 25% profit sharing and the next year there would be 50% profit sharing. This annual increase in profit sharing was to continue. In addition, the pay was to be $125.00 per week—a secret to be kept from his buddy in town who paid his pharmacist only $100 per week. This sounded great.

I took my State Board examination, passed and began working in 1953. This was a unique experience to say the least. State and Federal guidelines were not adhered to in a lot of businesses but I was plainly informed that if I did not concur with the in-house protocols, the information would be discussed with the clerk. I later learned that she would give the customers whatever they wanted. Every employee who worked there knew this policy. I remember very well the cigar box that contained "over-the-counter" prescriptions that were usually copies of Drs. Bagley and Claytor's originals. These were used with discretion.

Rifles, shotguns, switchblades, prepackaged penicillin were all sold randomly. As the first year drew to a close, I asked for a weekend off work to attend the University of Michigan homecoming football game and my request was granted. When I returned to work after the weekend, I was asked, "Where were you yesterday?" and I responded, "At the homecoming in Ann Arbor." I was then asked, "Can we make it, working together?" and I responded, "Do you want to make it work?"

Then I was advised that I had better leave (there was approximately $3,500 to $5,000 in the kitty by this time, all up for grabs)! I responded, "This must be racial," and soon thereafter I left. He hired Marv Stuekel from Davis Drugs, a male older than I who also saw this job as a chance for store ownership. I learned later that Marv received the same treatment I had. This was not racially motivated, it was just irrational. Time for another paradigm shift?

So, Bill Haithco was without a job … but not for long. I was informed that I should call the Saginaw Community Hospital as they were looking for a part-time pharmacist to work from 8 a.m. until noon, five days a week. I responded to Dr. V. K. Volk who had read about me several times in the Saginaw News and I was hired for the job. Dr. Volk at the time was our Saginaw County Health Doctor. Saginaw Community Hospital was our tuberculosis and contagious disease hospital. I learned shortly after my hiring that the former pharmacist had an affinity for "barley corn" and he was removed from duty.

In this hospital, patients did not receive prescriptions directly for their use, but floor stock of medications was delivered to the units, often in the manufacturer's containers, to be administered by staff. I had to prepare the surgery suite with "Tibbie" Cain who was the surgical nurse on the days that surgery was scheduled. Our surgeons typically came from Detroit. Soon after accepting this job, Ralph Radenbaugh, our Parke-Davis representative, told me that Harry Gunther wanted me to stop by his pharmacy on North Michigan Avenue some day as I left the hospital.

About a week later, I stopped by for a visit with Harry and his wife. They were sitting at the soda fountain. One of our neighbors, Joyce Green, was also sitting at the counter. Harry looked at me and said, "Are you Bill Haithco, the son of the man who used to work for the Schott Drugstore downtown years ago?" and I replied, "Yes". I was asked to take off my coat and get to work. He said he and his wife loved to fish and that they were going to East Tawas and fish. He said H & P would call for an order, he showed me the want book, the door locks, and gave me the store keys. He checked the Sterno stock and said for me to add six cases of Sterno to the order. Sterno (also known as canned heat) used a methyl alcohol in a jelly base and was often used as heat for chafing dishes. Four or five blocks from the Gunther Drugstore was the city dump where the derelicts, also called tramps, lived. They would come into the drugstore and buy Sterno and a bottle of water. I was advised that they had a method of straining the gel through bread (methyl alcohol can cause blindness) … these tramps were very learned. So I started working every Wednesday so that Harry and his wife could go fishing.

I married Nancy Fisher-Benjamin-Cobb in 1955 at the home of her parents in Detroit, Michigan. In June 1956, my son William Harold II was born and in 1957 my daughter Shari Lin was born. We lived in a two-room apartment at 3431-1/2 Rust Street. This apartment was shared with Jack and Marion Nash. I then became the first black pharmacist in the history of Saginaw and it didn't take long before Florence Porterfield called and said she had seen an empty building on Lapeer Street that might make a good location for my business.

Tell you what I want to tell you, then tell you, then tell you what I told you. Now the rest of the book—telling you like it is ... about the trials, tribulations, prejudices; the Princings, The Nisleys, the Auxiliary, the Girl Scouts, the Loobies, the Kents, the Lanes, the Frank Anderson Bowlingbar, the Morley school principal, the Grekel Greens, the Sturms, the churches, Credit Union employees, the Klaczkiewics, Loncynskis, the Harold Karls, Bob Grants, the Schultzes and the Beyers.

Tell me not in mournful numbers,
Life is but an empty dream;
For the soul is dead that slumbers,
And things are not what they seem.

On July 1, 1970, at the Michigan Pharmacists summer convention at Boyne Mountain Resort, I was awarded the Bowl of Hygeia Award by the A. H. Robins Company of Richmond, Virginia. This award was given to one pharmacist in each state and Puerto Rico. Each year this award was given for Outstanding Community Service in Pharmacy. With this award my picture appeared in the local community and TIME magazine "We, too, salute you".

"The A. H. Robins Bowl of Hygeia Award is an acknowledgement of your outstanding contributions to community life, over and above your professional duty as a member of the health team."

"To have been cited for such meritorious service, indicating both civic and professional responsibility, is a great honor. To have been selected for this distinction by your colleagues makes the honor even greater, for they are in the best position to assess impartially your worth in both areas."

"We add our congratulations. And we would like to express our pleasure in having the 'Bowl of Hygeia' recipients honored as a group in TIME ... 'the magazine to the leadership community.'"

The Kents

Ralph Kent had a drugstore on Wadsworth and Ninth Streets. One day he called me to tell me he was doing the annual remodeling of his store and he asked me to help him with this activity. Ralph would, almost annually, move items from one side of the pharmacy to the opposite side of the store. What he wanted me to do was help install the valance above the shelving that surrounded the inside of the store, rebuild the shelves, install lighting behind the valances and a variety of other non-pharmacist tasks. Many of the customers, salesmen, and doctors who patronized the pharmacy knew me and would stop to talk to me while I was helping with the "rearranging" of the store. Some of these people asked Ralph why he did not hire me as a pharmacist. After two weeks, Ralph asked me to come on board as a pharmacist ... what a good idea. Ralph was a good facilitator, promoter and the retired Joe Lane was his pharmacist. I accepted the position and worked for Ralph from 2 p.m. to 10 p.m. daily. From 8 a.m. until about noon, I would still work at Saginaw Community Hospital. This was in 1954. Oh, what a welcome.

Ralph and his wife, Helen, were very lovely people, were very community conscious, and very liberal minded. They belonged to Pit and Balcony, Tuesday Musical, and other cultural groups. I accepted the job offer and became a pill counter and stopped pounding nails for the "annual reorganization." But there were people in the community who did not think like Ralph and Helen. They expressed feelings when they cut an article from the paper and where the article mentioned the word "pharmacist" they wrote above the word "nigger". This was a changing neighborhood and there was some rejection. But Ralph did not care. I would take a bottle of 500 tablets, dump some out into the counting tray, and tell the concerned customer there were 107 or 102 tablets on the tray. Most of the time I was very accurate.

While I was filling the prescription, Ralph would get a fishing fly rod, hook a dummy plug on the fishing line, and show the customer how he could cast the plug and hit the knob on the front door that was 30 feet away. Ralph was a very good fly fisherman and loved to catch and eat fresh trout, head and all.

Ralph did not own the building where the pharmacy was located but there was a barbershop and Dork's Grocery Store next door. All contained in the same building. Joe Eimers owned the building and had the barbershop between the pharmacy and the grocery store. Joe lived upstairs. One day Ralph asked me if I knew a black doctor who would come to Saginaw and practice in the building where Joe had his barbershop. I knew a black doctor, Walter L. Webb, who was a student at the University of Michigan in Ann Arbor when I attended pharmacy school. I knew Walter was interning in Lansing, Michigan, and I went there to talk to him about Saginaw. After some deliberation and a trip to Saginaw, Dr. Webb decided to move to Saginaw and in with Ralph Kent to occupy a building at 1502 Wadsworth.

Earl and Mildred Keene had a home on North Seventh Street and offered Dr. Webb a place to stay in their home. At that point in my life, I decided I always believed in education as a driver in helping the economy and helping society as a whole, thereby improving the quality of life for all concerned. The point of living is not to see how much money you can make. The point and my thrust is to do something to improve the quality of life for people.

Ralph Kent was a very nice person to work for and with. Not only a good humorist, but also a concerned person. One night after the annual pharmacist, dentist, and doctor party at the Shrine Temple, Ralph, Sig Johnson, Ralph Radenbaugh, and I decided to go to Frank Anderson's bowling bar on South Fourth Street behind Davis Drugs (Boyden Davis was with us also). As I was about to sit down, the waitress held my chair and said, "Sorry, we cannot serve you". I knew then that I was the "wrong color". So Ralph responded, "Well, let's go to my pharmacy and I will buy everyone a night cap". So we left.

Ralph had two sons, Gerry and Bill, both of whom were in pharmacy school at that time. I had just been released from employment at Kent Drugstore, as Ralph had to make room in the family business for Gerry, who had four children and a wife Pat (Pegley) to support. This he clearly explained to all present as he made me ring up the sale for the McNaughton's. Bill Kent was dating Lou Hatchel from Bay City and we would frequently double date. Bill and Lou liked the night clubs on John R. Street in Detroit and one night as we were leaving Club 666, the bar maid said "Hello, Ms. Benjamin" to my date. I was surprised, but that was life.

I stopped in to talk with Russ Princing, of Princing and Brennan Pharmacy, about the possibility of hiring me in his pharmacy at Janes and Fourteenth Streets and he said he did not have enough black customers to warrant hiring me. About this time, Edna Lane, wife of pharmacist Joe Lane, asked my wife to join the Pharmacists Auxiliary with the first meeting at the Richer's home on East Genesee Street. At this meeting one of the attendees rose up in righteous indignation at having to eat with the same place settings as my wife! WELL HELLO! Now everything got sour. This was the end for the wife's membership.

Ralph Kent was a very concerned person and at times some of us thought he may not have been concerned enough. But Ralph at some point in time had the opinion that he might have been "short" some money so he began keeping track of the daily cash register tapes on a stenographer pad. On his chosen day, he chose to call me at the hospital and ask me when I got home and before I went to the pharmacy would I please call the Ford Bail Bond Agency and ask them to send one of their agents to the Kent Pharmacy for some "orientation".

Ralph had noticed the register to be OVER on many days. He noted the days and the amounts of overages. Then on certain days, this overage would show up as a shortage! Ralph called me in early one day to talk to me. Being the only black employee, I had been told by Mom that I would always be the first suspect if anything ever went wrong. I did not feel guilty but I felt I had to tell the truth. Ralph's so called "manager" from 6 p.m. until closing at 10 p.m. was a childhood "buddy", and they drank beer together and fished together quite often. Redd worked at a local wholesale candy and tobacco distributor and thought he would like working for Ralph evenings. This way he could get $2.00 per hour and save $10.00 by not going to the bar every night.

At the interrogation I asked Ralph, "Who was the one who always kept the cash drawer open during the night?" This involved making change from the register drawer without ringing the amount of the sale. Every night at 6 p.m., when Redd came to work, he would go right to that register at the back southeast corner of the store and do something! What I did not know. About once a week, when he came to the pharmacy and Ralph was gone, he would go to the phone, call someone named Babe and they would discuss his (Babe's) order. "You are short one box of El Producto cigars, three cartons of cigarettes, one package of Doublemint® gum." "O.K., I'll bring them right over and I'll replace Ralph's stock." There were nights when this Babe would call Redd at the store and in very muffled tones there would be a conversation. In a few minutes, Redd would say to me as he walked out of the store, "I'll be right back". There would be a box over his head that may have contained three, four, or five fifths of whiskey going to this "friend". Money order funds were often short or blank money orders were missing. At one point in time, Ralph even changed the money order company he dealt with!

The investigative agency made numerous purchases for cash that no one knew about. Ralph loved trout fishing and sold much fishing gear. One evening a person walked into the pharmacy and made a purchase of an expensive fishing reel and paid cash in the exact amount including sales tax. No, the sale was not registered and there stood Redd with his pants down (too much money in the pockets).

The next day, Ralph called me to say his childhood buddy had been caught. The agents noted the time of purchase, amount of the purchase, and the item purchased. No receipt was given and there was no sales register tape! Ralph was notified and in one day Ralph contacted me for advice. There were probably "thousands of dollars" involved over a period of four or five years. Who knows?

I was very glad it was all over. I guess I always said, "That's his best friend from early childhood and he's white and white is always right ... wrong." The next day or so Ralph talked to me and said, "We were friends for many years. Played together, fished together. What should I do? We are supposed to go fishing up at the Lovells the next weekend and if I wait until then and get him out in the river in the boat and break the news to him, he is bigger than I and he might dump me into the river." I do not remember how Ralph resolved this issue, but I don't believe they went up north to fish. Perhaps Mary Kent Sullivan will remember this result. This will end this little "vignette" as I was soon to be released from duty as Gerry Kent, Ralph's first son and husband of Mary Kent Sullivan graduated from Ferris State University and Ralph had to make room for Gerry in the business. Family comes first! But, don't worry, I will be back! If you love someone and set them free, they shall return one day to thee!

I looked for a vacant house on Lapeer Street but couldn't find the one Florence Porterfield had referred to. But I did see a building on Wadsworth at 12th Street that was "For Sale." It was the Joe Lonczynski Barber Shop, at 1800 Wadsworth Street, where Joe and his wife Mabel and daughter lived with the barber/beauty shop in the front and they lived in the back. I bought the house for $8,500 on land contract and my father and I were in the remodeling business. I had the city school patrol officer, Chet Parkin, make some Schwartz cabinets and shelving for me. Dad and I cut out the front windows to make them "store" size and ordered a new front door. Jack Dietz made outdoor signs for the side and front and I went to Hazeltine & Perkins wholesalers in Grand Rapids (Michigan) to see about getting an opening order. They told me to get whatever I wanted and to pay for it as I saw fit. WOW!

We moved the family in and completed the establishment of the Haithco Prescription Pharmacy. Our little apartment consisted of a small "living room," one bedroom, a small bathroom and a small kitchen. Just enough room for the four of us! After living at the pharmacy for three years, I was able to build a new home in 1960, the same year my son Jai Spencer was born. Business was good and I was able to continue my work at the Saginaw Community Hospital in the mornings until noon.

Nancy would run the store until I arrived. All this was fine until one very nice, kind, and loving person turned me in to the State Board of Pharmacy for not having a pharmacist on duty when the pharmacy was open, even though Nancy did not fill prescriptions in my absence! So, the days of "guaranteed" income were over and I had to resign my position at County Hospital. Doctors were very supportive of my presence in the community and soon I was asked to join the Saginaw Chamber of Commerce.

The first year on the Chamber, I was asked to serve on the membership committee. And, in that capacity, I brought in the most new members for the first prize. The prize was a three-day vacation for two, which I have not taken as yet!

Community Drugs

In the mid 60s, Jimmie Krohn and Wallace Strobel came to me one day and they said they had an idea. The idea was a mail order prescription pharmacy at 1800 Wadsworth, the same address as Haithco Prescription Pharmacy but a separate corporation. I thought this to be an excellent idea and I came up with the name "Community Benefit Drugs, Inc." We set up the necessary protocols for a corporation and wrote the Board of Pharmacy for permission to establish this business. Wally owned Central Warehouse and Jimmie owned Seitners Department Store.

An inspector came to Saginaw from Lansing and at separate times visited with Wallace Strobel, James Krohn, and me. I was subsequently informed that the State of Michigan denied the license because there was no law on the books covering such a business.

6

Community Involvement

Big Brothers and Big Sisters

With this in mind, I adopted what I call "the Haithco habit" which was to say "Yes" to any request asked of me, to be a part of any venue that would improve the quality of life of others, and that was by all means practical and feasible. If no one needs you, what good are you? To thine own self be true and thou cannot be false to any man. And with these thoughts in mind, I answered the call and joined Big Brothers of America, an organization of men who are dedicated to helping male children in need of help outside of their own families. This may have included a home where there was no father or a home with a father who could not be a father or a friend. Big Sisters of America is the organization that exists to provide the same type of support to females. This organization provided many happy moments and my little brother Bobbie and I made his sister a wooden cradle for one Christmas, which Bobby had established as his primary goal of our interactions.

Junior Achievement

My next call to duty was to join the Junior Achievement program of Saginaw. This was a program for high school students to learn the protocols, principles, and practices of a good business. The program was designed to help the student form his own corporation/company, elect officers, and choose a product to manufacture, design a marketing campaign and embark on a targeted sales program.

The Junior Achievement (JA) program was a wonderful program for the student, for the camaraderie and the experiences that it offered. I still have three to four former students who are very friendly toward me. Our chosen name was HaGoGem Company as it was sponsored by the Haithco Prescription Pharmacy, Godwin Printing Company and General Motors.

Dan Schutt was our president, Martha Cederberg was our secretary and I believe Joe Kelly was our treasurer. Occasionally, I would stop in to see Dan at his store in Ann Arbor after he was grown. He specialized in jade; his business was located at the corner of Huron and State Streets, in Ann Arbor, Michigan.

Model Cities

Henry Marsh came to Saginaw in the late 50s to set up practice as an attorney. Mr. Marsh soon became our mayor and in 1967 Saginaw was named a Model City by the federal government. The designation was given because of the Saginaw program to increase open housing and improve race relations. I was on the Mayor's Committee of Concern and Mr. Marsh appointed me to the Model City Committee, which I named the Model City Involvement Committee. It was from this affiliation that I learned there were federal funds available for such venues as golf courses and tennis courts if the chosen area was near an urban setting.

There was an airport in Buena Vista Township across from Saginaw Steering Gear that was owned by the City of Saginaw. It was 145 acres of "paid for" property that the city owned. There were six or seven golf courses in Saginaw County but all were privately owned and none were on the east side of the county. All offered open service to the public. Dr. Barnes, Charlie Kench, Jim Granse, and I would on occasion go out to Green Acres at 5 a.m. in the morning and play a fast nine holes of golf and get back in town in time for work at 9 a.m. But this was south of Bridgeport (Michigan). On a certain Saturday morning in the fall of 1968, Attorney Henry Marsh, our Mayor, invited City Manager Ed Potthoff and his wife, and me and my wife to go to Ann Arbor for the University of Michigan football game. When we were riding past Holland Road in Henry's motor home, I asked Ed Potthoff if the city made any money off of the City Airport.

His answer was "No," and it cost the city of Saginaw money to maintain the facility. There was little business use and some flight training services. I was, and still am, a person who would not resign myself to a position of innocuous desuetude and I embarked on a program to provide a Municipal Golf Course on the east side of Saginaw County. The first in the history of Saginaw County.

I had petitions signed by citizens in Saginaw County as they visited my pharmacy, or as I saw them in our community as I visited our schools, churches, public meetings, etc. Dr. Barnes, Attorney Marsh and Bill Haithco were members of the Optimist Club and when the representative of Optimist International came to Saginaw to charge the new Breakfast Optimist Club, we three were all Black members. Hello! Some of the members of the Optimist Club also circulated petitions for the golf course.

The Saginaw News printed an editorial in the paper in support of my idea and the Chamber of Commerce also lent support to the golf course project. I would periodically send petitions to Liz Donaldson, City Clerk, as I had them signed. By May 17, 1969, a total of 976 names had been submitted to the City of Saginaw. On July 23, 1969, Howard Sheltraw of the City Planning Commission advised me that the city could not requisition these funds from the federal government through the governor of Michigan. The funds for recreational and conservational purposes must be obtained by the County of Saginaw or its official organ.

Golf Course Letter Dated 8–12–69

Petition originally submitted to City Council of Saginaw on March 17, 1969, for building of golf course on east side of Saginaw, a recommended municipal course (or whatever city would deem feasible).

One suggested site was that of the Janes Street Airport, as the city of Saginaw already owns this 160-acre parcel of property. At intervals additional names were added to original petition and on May 17, 1969 173 names were finally added to bring the total of concerned citizens to 976.

Upon submission of last lists of names, request was made to City Council to seek a portion of $100 million dollars granted to the State of Michigan for recreational and conservation purposes.

By article in Saginaw News of 7–22–679 golf courses are given a priority in the recreation area. Action MUST be taken by Board of Supervisors and County Planning Commission soon in order to take advantage of available funds.

Mr. Haithco was advised on 7–23–69 by Mr. Sheltraw, City Planning Commission, that the City of Saginaw could NOT requisition these funds available from the federal government through the governor of Michigan. These funds for recreational and conservational purposes must be obtained by the COUNTY of Saginaw or its official organ.

With this in mind, Mr. Haithco immediately began seeking help from Mr. Crampton and the County Board of Supervisors. It is thought that a recreational venture as a golf course on the east side of Saginaw could well include in "package form" possibly a park facility, camping area, picnic site (or sites) and any other recreational facilities deemed to be desirable and of utility to the GREATER SAGINAW area.

Such a facility MUST and WILL serve ALL the residents (and travelers) of Saginaw and its peripheral area of residence, e.g., Buena Vista, Highland Park, Downs, Birch Run, Reese, Frankenmuth, Richville, Indiantown, Munger, Bridgeport, Spaulding, etc. Somewhere there is a need ... somewhere there is a desire ... somewhere there is a dream. (The list of names of those who have shown a desire is in the hands of the City Clerk and I am sure I could obtain it on request.)

Parks and Recreation

On August 6, 1969, I wrote the Saginaw County Board of Supervisors asking them to form a Saginaw County Parks and Recreation Commission under Public Act 261 and on August 29, 1969, I received a letter from Julius Sutto, County Controller.

I contacted Marvin Crampton and the County Board of Supervisors and asked them to form a Parks and Recreation Commission. In September 1969, the Saginaw County Board of Supervisors established the Saginaw County Parks and Recreation Commission. Said commission was established pursuant to Act 261 of the Public Acts of the State of Michigan of 1965, as amended.

COUNTY of SAGINAW
Office of the
COUNTY CONTROLLER   COUNTY CONTROLLER

COURT HOUSE   SAGINAW, MICHIGAN

August 29, 1969

Mr. William H. Haithco
1800 Wadsworth
Saginaw, Michigan

Dear Mr. Haithco:

Your letter of August 6, 1969, addressed to Mr. Prahm,
Chairman of the Board of Supervisors, was referred to
the Committee on Highways and County Affairs.

Your letter received the thoughtful consideration of the
Committee and the conclusion was reached that in light
of the ever increasing need for recreational facilities
in Saginaw County, it appears desirable to pursue the
creation of an official board through which parks and
recreation programs and facilities can be developed.

Accordingly, the Committee at the September 9 session
of the Board will offer a resolution creating a Saginaw
County Parks and Recreation Commission to implement the
above mentioned objectives.

Your letter will be referred to the newly created
Commission and I am sure will receive proper consideration.

Very truly yours,

Julius Sutto,
County Controller

JS/sr

30 years later—1999

The letter below dated November 24, 1987 from Lucy R. Allen, President, CEO, Saginaw Community Foundation summarizes our efforts to establish a fund to ensure that the parks would be funded by donations to a non-government agency. Contributions were requested from General Motors a letter from C. E. White, Chairman, GM—Saginaw Public Affairs Committee, dated 2–17–88, denied request for contribution to the Saginaw County Parks Fund. However, on 12–21–88 GM contributed $5,000 toward flooding Hoyt Park and providing evening supervision.

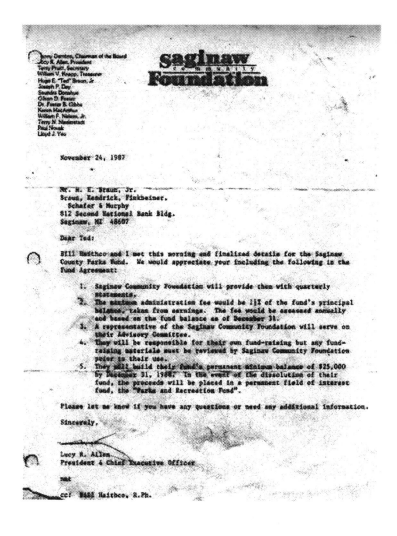

In 1956, Imerman Memorial Park was given to Saginaw County by Dr. and Mrs. Louis A. Imerman in honor of his deceased brother, Attorney Elliott Imerman. J.C.'s later received this site consisting of 96 acres, including 34,750 feet of frontage along the Tittabawassee River, and in February 1971, Imerman Memorial Park was given to the Saginaw County Parks and Recreation Commission.

In 1978, MSU decided to sell the property named Price Forest and in October 1978, I began correspondence and dialogue with the late Jack Breslin, Executive Vice President of Michigan State University (MSU) and Starr Keesler, Executive V.P. for Administration of MSU. In February 1979, I took DPW Director Jim Clark to East Lansing to meet with Breslin and Keesler. Price Forest (136 acres) was given to MSU Forestry Department on September 23, 1940, by James C. and Emily Johns Price, to preserve the area as a memorial forest. MSU decided to sell said property for the appraised price of $114,500.

We had $100,000 in revenue funds from County General Fund and I recommended to the SCPR Land Acquisition Committee that we purchase subject parcel for $100,000. And MSU accepted. At its June meeting, Bob Presprich moved we name the park the William H. Haithco Memorial Park.

Bob Bolger said, "We should reconsider, maybe someone else deserves credit," and Tom Kochendorfer said, "Perhaps we could name a building in the future after Haithco". I referred (by a motion) the issue to Price Nature Center Advisory Council. At its meeting of the Advisory Council on July 16, 1979, with opposition from Chairman Albert Boelter, Harvey Wilson, Alice Schiesswohl, and input from Nancy Austin Schwartz (later to become Governor Blanchard's Deputy Chief for External Affairs), the Advisory Council voted "No" on the name change. The Advisory Council directed Jim Clark to call me the next day and see if I would feel bad if they did not name the park after me. My answer was, "No, I am not surprised at the decision. Is it because of 'what I am'?" to which Clark replied, "Yes, and the location … Bridgeport."

Price Nature Center is now 186 acres and opened officially in 1981. It is now a popular hiking, picnic, cross-country skiing and nature study area offering 3.5 miles of hiking and nature trails with group campsites. Development funding has been provided by the Michigan Department of Natural Resources, the Wickes Foundation (Jimmy), and Second National Bank Trust Department.

A letter dated November 4, 1977, from Jackie Ivanhoff, a girl scout leader from Flushing, Michigan, expressed gratitude to Jamie (staff member) for his help when a girl scout troup visited the Price Nature Center. Ms. Ivanhoff repeatedly indicated how important it was to offer new experiences to youngsters within their home communities.

Ringwood Forest

On November 20, 1930, an Indenture between Clark L. Ring, a widower, of Saginaw, and the Regents of The University of Michigan, a constitutional corporation, was prepared, and was signed and witnessed on November 21, 1930, said Indenture covering sale of land in the Township of Brant, City of Saginaw, State of Michigan for "one dollar and other valuable considerations".

The property was to be maintained and planted to timber, as recommended by the School of Forestry and Conservation of The University of Michigan, to the end that it may be maintained as a reservation for the promotion of the study of forestry. This was the beginning of what came to be known as Ringwood Forest.

Almost 50 years later, on April 2, 1980, my letter to Prof. Douglas A. MacKinnon, Chairman, Properties Committee, of the School of Natural Resources at The University of Michigan, expressed my desire to see "Ringwood," the most beautiful undeveloped natural site in the Saginaw County, become an integral part of the County Parks and Recreation system. Since the terms of the Clark L. Ring Estate did not allow for The University of Michigan to sell the property, I proposed a long-term lease agreement for a period of from 30 to 50 years.

On July 3, 1980, Professor MacKinnon replied that my proposal could be of some interest to the School of Natural Resources, at least as a starting point for discussing ways to work together to accomplish the somewhat different objectives the two organizations have, and indicating it would have to wait until late September, when the Properties Board would have its first meeting after the summer break. His personal feelings were to intensify forest management there with the objective of maximizing timber production, thus producing some annual income to offset expenses involved in operating other properties, but he suggested this approach need not be incompatible with low-density recreational use or outdoor education.

A memo from John D. Ketelhut, Office of the General Counsel, The University of Michigan, raised the question whether the lease for park facilities would be a breach of the condition in the Warranty Deed that the property be maintained as a forest reserve, which could result in the property's reverting to the grantor or his heirs. He suggested that the compatibility of the lease with the other uses of the property would have to be explored and further analyzed. He also pointed out that rental charges for the use of land for sponsored research projects was specifically excluded, although charges for operating costs, such as a caretaker, might be possible.

My letter of March 24, 1981, to James D. Ireland, one of three heirs of the Ring Estate, conveyed the plans of the Saginaw County Parks and Recreation Commission and The University of Michigan in developing "Ringwood" as a source of low-profile recreation activity and for forestry research and instruction programs, suggesting it would be helpful if he and the other two heirs would concur with the thinking and desires of the Commission and The University to see this development reach fruition. Mr. Ireland acknowledged receipt of the information on March 30, 1981, indicating he would be out of the country until early May, but was sending copies on to the other heirs for their consideration.

On May 1, 1981, Mr. Ireland wrote that their files did not contain any information about Ringwood, and that he suspected it was given to The University of Michigan by a separate document rather than through the estate files. He and the other heirs were especially interested to know if there was a reversionary clause in the document in the event The University of Michigan failed to continue to use the land, but said not to be alarmed, because the heirs would look with favor on a proper usage of the land.

In a letter dated January 28, 1982, Charles E. Olson, Jr., Professor of Natural Resources at The University of Michigan describes a visit to "Ringwood" which uncovered some unauthorized tree cutting and some vandalism that would need correction, but added that developing the property as an educational/recreation area would bring more people to the property, and if their experience was good it would decrease the vandalism. If it was bad, it could increase such problems. He felt close collaboration with the Saginaw County Parks and Recreation staff could provide the good experiences everyone wanted.

A meeting between the current Chairman of the Properties Board of The University of Michigan and myself was proposed by John A. Scholtz, Director of the Saginaw County Parks and Recreation Commission, for February 26, 1982, in Ann Arbor to discuss the status of the Commission's request for a possible lease of the Ringwood property.

In my October 14, 1982 letter to James D. Ireland I enclosed a copy of the proposed lease for "Ringwood". It also included a Project Description, including park development to include a variety of year-round uses by development of several facilities: entry drives and parking, canoe access point, main gate and general signing, picnic area with rustic restrooms, well and play equipment, interpretive exhibit with environmental education displays, extensive trail development, bridge repair, sledding hill contouring and other miscellaneous items. It also included a Project Schedule that began in January 1980 with the original recommendation to acquire the site, and would end in September 1985 with the Ringwood Forest "Grand Opening".

On January 4, 1983, I wrote James D. Ireland that we were now ready to have the lease formally adopted by The University of Michigan and the Saginaw County Board of Commissioners.

On September 14, 1983, John A. Scholtz, Director of the Saginaw County Parks and Recreation Committee, wrote to Don Kiel, Administrative Manager of the U of M School of Natural Resources, to suggest an October 28 meeting at the Ringwood property to hike the site and discuss its future. The meeting would be with Don Kiel, Chuck Olson, John and me.

On November 3, 1983, I wrote James D. Ireland about the good news! Late in the summer the University had formally approved the lease agreement providing the Parks Commission use of the property for thirty years at one dollar per year! The plan was to work through the winter to raise $30,000 to accomplish the work of establishing a site plan for development of the parking area, restrooms, picnic area, trails, educational displays, and other facilities. Operating funds would come from the County, but it was necessary to raise the development funds.

On February 3, 1984, I wrote to Mr. Robert Bierlein, of Bierlein Demolition Contractors, soliciting a "donation of service" in clearing an area 160' x 50' for a parking area. We would pay the cost of gas and oil if they would supply the equipment and manpower. On February 10, 1984, Gary Bierlein, President, responded that they would be most happy to provide a front-end loader or dozer for the proposed "Ringwood" development.

The Ringwood Forest Advisory Council met on February 9, 1984 in the Brant Township Hall. Chairman Kochendorfer and 12 Council members were present, along with John Scholtz, myself, and 25 local residents.

John Scholtz presented background information regarding the Parks and Recreation Commission. I reviewed the history of the Ringwood site and the negotiations with The University of Michigan, resulting in the long-term lease of the site. The lease terms were reviewed to make the Advisory Council aware of restrictions and rights placed on the Park Commission's use of the site, and also the rights to use retained by The University of Michigan. Kochendorfer explained the Advisory Council role in preparation of a long-range master plan for the site.

Scholtz reviewed the master plan process, and then presented the preliminary site plan for the Ringwood Forest that was approved by The University and Parks

Commission. The plan was not limited as presented but could be revised and expanded to show long-range plans. After discussion, Advisory Council members expressed support for the site plan as a first phase development. Submission of a grant application, based on the preliminary site plan and an approximate cost of $40,000, to the Land and Water Conservation Fund, with a filing deadline of March 31, 1984, was voted and approved.

Several members of the audience expressed concern over policing of the site, upkeep of the park and set park hours with established closing times. Those in attendance were urged to visit the Price Nature Center in the Bridgeport area, where local residents had raised the same questions, but had since become supporters of the park.

The actual Pre-Application, dated March 1, 1984, was for a grant in the amount of $26,500 or 50% of the $53,000 project cost.

A letter dated April 25, 1984, from Charles W. Cares, Professor of Landscape Architecture & Regional Planning, U of M, to John Scholtz proposed using the services of Wendy Fry, who had agreed to work on the project. She would carry out the analysis, prepare the program and plan, and secure feedback from the Parks and Recreation Commission. She would make drawings and perform all other tasks associated with the work. The final product would be in the form of a report, which would include a plan setting forth the elements and would present the rationale for the plan.

The work would include at least one formal presentation to the entire committee or community, as appropriate. The cost would be $2,500.

A letter dated July 17, 1984 from James F. Cleary, Assistant Director and Liaison Officer for the Department of Natural Resources, State of Michigan, informed John Scholtz that the pre-application for Land and Water Conservation Fund assistance was recommended for funding at the level requested. All necessary forms and information were enclosed and the deadline for the full application was August 31, 1984.

A Proposal for the Ringwood Forest Development Project was sent to Second National Bank Trust Department on August 1, 1984. The "Saginaw County Parks Recreation and Open Space Plan" completed in 1980 identified the southwest portion of Saginaw County as top priority for park acquisition. Of the sites studied, Ringwood Forest was rated top priority for acquisition. A review of the site and its resources showed it to be capable of meeting several long-range goals:

- Provide an important day-use area meeting county-wide recreation needs.

- Provide a wide range of recreational activities within a ½ hour drive of 87% of the county's population.

- Offer year-round recreation potential (i.e., winter activities, cross-country skiing, sledding hill, hiking, etc.)

- Provide water-based recreation opportunities with access to the Bad River

- Expand environmental education programs.

- Preserve fragile flood plain areas and protects rare plant and animal communities.

- Protect important county historical area (i.e., site of State's first pine plantation).

The Project Budget Expenditures amounted to $53,000, covering facility construction, professional fees, and contingencies. Revenues expected included $26,5600 from a State Grant, $12,000 from the County Parks Budget, a total of $38,500. The Foundation Request from the Second National Bank Trust Fund was for $14,500.

Attachments to the proposal included a location map, detailed preliminary cost estimates, site development plan, infrared aerial photo of site, and a copy of property lease from the University of Michigan.

In my letter to James D. Ireland dated August 16, 1984, I enclosed pertinent information regarding the development of "Ringwood". I also explained that County funds are not available for this low-profile development, but I planned to go to the volunteer and "private sectors" for funding in order to develop this choice recreational property. James acknowledged receipt of the information on September 17.

On July 5, 1986, I wrote E. Peter Garrett, one of the three Ring heirs, suggesting a meeting on July 17 in Seattle. Apparently Mr. Garrett was out of town and did not receive my invitation. Letters from Mr. Garrett and James D. Ireland, dated January 29, 1987 and January 28, 1987 respectively, both indicate they feel Clark L. Ring would have been very happy with the use of his land.

James D. Ireland acknowledged on June 15, 1987, receipt of an invitation to the Dedication of Ringwood Forest on June 21, 1987. It mentions that work on this project began in 1980! It also refers to a plaque at the site that showed the land to be part of the great Pine Forest of Michigan lumbered in 1862 by Ebenezer W. Ring and where one of the earliest forest plantations in the States was established in 1883 by his son, Clark L. Ring, in memory of his brother, William

L. Ring, in a presentation to The University of Michigan in 1930. He and Peter Garrett were very pleased to be a part of making this possible.

In subsequent letters from James D. Ireland in March and April 1990, he expresses appreciation for the clippings from the Saginaw News about Ringwood Forest that I sent him from time to time.

Peter Garrett at Ringwood

After completion of I-75, the Michigan Highway Department found it no longer feasible to maintain the Veterans Memorial Park located between the Saginaw River and M-13. In 1971, the Saginaw County Parks and Recreation Commission acquired this three-acre, approximately 3.5 mile long site. As this site did not offer much depth for development and we acquired the site for $5.00, the price was right. Highlight of development was the completion of the boat launch in 1982, with the help of the Department of Natural Resources Waterways Division.

In early 1980, a spot on the map of Saginaw was noted as "State of Michigan" and was found to be the University of Michigan.

Across from the 160-acre site was a sign: "Ringwood," and in the drain ditch was a rock with a brass plate mentioning names of three Ring persons. This site was south of St. Charles (Michigan) and I told Director John Scholtz to go back and see if by chance one of the names was "Clark L. Ring" ... it was there and the inscription read "Eleazer J. Ring lumbered this land, originally a part of the great Pine Forest of Michigan, in 1862. Here one of the earliest forest plantations in the state of Michigan was established in 1883 by his son William Lee Ring, in whose memory his brother, Clark, presented the tract to the University of Michigan in 1930, to be used henceforth for instruction, demonstration, and research in forestry."

Through Dr. Ara G. Paul, Dean of the University of Michigan School of Pharmacy, I was able to meet and talk with Donald Keil, Administrative Manager of the School of Natural Resources on March 28, 1980, to discuss my intentions to acquire said property for Saginaw County Parks. I had a dialogue with another friend of Dr. Ara G. Paul, Professor Douglas A. MacKinnon, then Chairman of the Property Committee, and eventually met with MacKinnon on July 3, 1980. Approximately November 5, 1980, Charles E. Olson, Jr., new Chairman of the Property Board, contacted John D. Ketelhut of the University of Michigan Office of General Counsel for Interpretation of Terms of Transfer of Title ... a long-term lease was the goal. I had to find a living heir to change terms of use of Ringwood. (Photo of Peter Garrett and Hope Ryan)

On or about March 9, 1981, E. Peter Garrett, grandson of Clark L. Ring, called to give his permission and that of his sister, to proceed with acquisition of property. After months and months of meetings between Saginaw County and U of M legal counsel, an agreement of $1.00 per year for 30 years was reached and the park officially opened in 1986, and was dedicated on Sunday, June 21, 1987. This 160-acre natural park is located in Brant Township, approximately 1.9 miles west of M-52 and the junction of Ring Road and Fordney Road. The south branch of the Bad River winds through this rolling heavily wooded site, featuring exceptional historic pine and spruce plantings. It is the site of the oldest formal pine planting in Michigan. It is perhaps the oldest in the United States as per the Department of Interior. Ringwood offers fishing, canoeing access, picnic tables, grills, picnic pavilion, rustic restrooms, children's play area, interpretive displays and 3.5 miles of self-guided nature/cross country ski trails/hiking. Mahatma* Gandhi once said "Consciously or unconsciously, every one of us does render some service or other. It we cultivate the habit of doing this service deliberately our desire for service will steadily grow stronger and will make not only our own happiness, but that of the world at large."

Saginaw County is the only county of 83 in Michigan that does not have a God-given lake, a natural lake. Since the first Parks Recreation and Open Space Plan, and in all subsequent five—and ten-year development plans, it has been listed a priority to provide a water-based recreation facility for the citizens of Saginaw County and its tourists. The ideal target site for this facility was the 33-acre S-H Lake in Saginaw Township between McCarty and Schust Roads at I-675.

This site was used as a "borrow" pit for fill dirt for the construction of I-675. Usually borrow pits are clay in nature. But this beautiful body of water was and is spring fed and very clear water, excellent for development. After construction of I-675 was completed, the site became the property of Saginaw Township.

Saginaw Township and Saginaw County for a number of years were not on the best "speaking terms". The township wanted the county 40 acres on Hospital Road next to the Receiving Home and the county wanted 32.8 acres fronting McCarty (including 25 acres surface water).

During the summer of 1986, we were told we could begin "talking" again and in October 1986, we arranged the "swap" of properties. County Government said County Parks and Recreation could develop subject property if we acquired the 39-acre parcel north of the Lake that was assessed at $330,000 by a group of South Haven attorneys and businessmen. The DNR provided their 75% and the county government, Wickets Foundation, Second National Trust Department, Morley Foundation, and Bill Haithco provided the needed 25%. In December 1986, the property was acquired.

In December 1987, Saginaw County Parks Fund was started by me as an endowment under the Saginaw Community Foundation to raise monies for all of Saginaw County Parks.

William H. Haithco Recreation Area
Under Construction

In November 1989, ground was broken for construction of the William H. Haithco Recreation Area, with a projected date of completion of July 4, 1990.

Beginning of Lake Haithco Ground Breaking

Bill on the Front Loader at Lake Haithco

Alice Schiesswohl and Bill Haithco

Pile Driving at Lake Haithco

Beginning of Lake Haithco

#3 Engineer for Phase III

Maybe we'll have a road?

Jim Blaschka over seeing the work at Lake Haithco

Bill by the Lake Haithco
The following photos are the construction and completion of the many facets the park offers.

The Park was stocked by the DNR with vast varieties of fish.

Building of the Pavillion

Finished Pavillion on Lake Haithco

LAKE HAITHCO

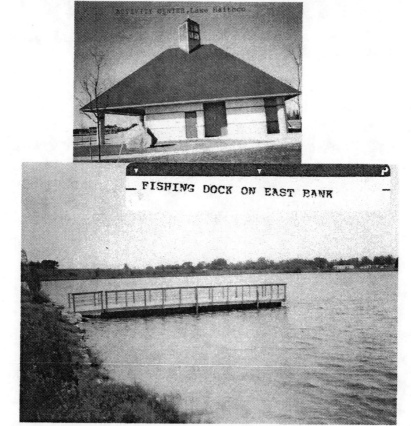

FISHING DOCK ON EAST BANK

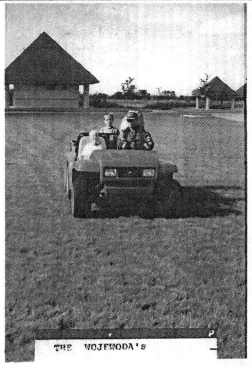

THE WOJEWODA'S

Dedication of William H. Haithco Recreation Area

Due to bad weather and soil conditions, opening was postponed, and Sunday, May 19, 1991, was selected as the date for dedication of the William H. Haithco Recreation Area at 2121 Schust Road. I picked Cullie Damuth and Patty Shaheen as Co-Chairpersons to work with Lucy Allen, Chairperson of the Saginaw Community Foundation, to work with me on the dedication program, the first of its type in the history of Saginaw County.

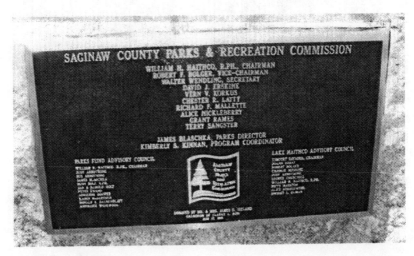

The William H. Haithco Recreation Area provides fishing, picnic tables, grills, picnic pavilions, modern restrooms, children's play area, swimming beach, sailboard beach, paddle boat rentals, concession stands, sand volleyball courts, scuba diving and is handicap accessible.

Indira Gandhi once said: "There are two kinds of people: those who do the work and those who take the credit. Try to be in the first group; there is less competition."

I wish to thank my family for sharing me with the community for thirty years and all of those having a part in the provision of recreational services to citizens of Saginaw County. I began planting flowers at the William H. Haithco Recreation Area about 1993 and I want to thank all those who have voluntarily taken over the upkeep of the flowers at Lake Haithco, Imerman Park, and Ringwood, especially Pat and Vern Korkus, Darwin, the Master Gardeners, and the Women's Farm and Garden members. I would also like to thank those Parks Commissioners who have raised money for the lovely plaque.

Paddle Boats Donated by Credit Union of Saginaw County

Sailing and Boating on the lake

103

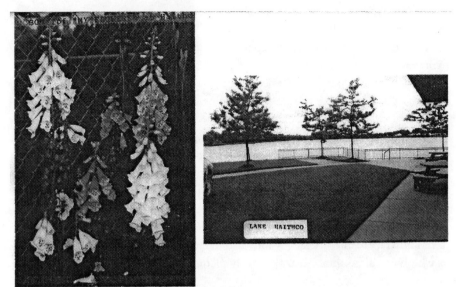

View from the Patio of the Pavillion

Entrance to the Park

A letter from the Saginaw County Board of Commissioners, dated June 21, 1990, indicates a donation of $8,500 was received from the Saginaw Valley Rotary Club to pay for construction of two pavilions at the William H. Haithco Recreation Area. This was the first installment of a $23,000 planned donation over a three-year period.

A five-page letter, dated January 8, 1996, from the Department of Natural Resources reports on the netting and electrofishing surveys conducted by Saginaw Bay District fisheries staff at Lake Haithco in October, 1995. The purpose was to assess the general health of the fish community and evaluate fishery management strategies. The conclusion was that the fish community of Lake Haithco is very healthy and shows no signs of excessive fishing pressure. The lake contains large-mouth bass, yellow perch, bullheads, northern pike, and catfish. The lake will be resurveyed and monitored from time to time.

On July 15, 1997, a letter was sent by Bill Haithco, Chairman of the Saginaw County Parks and Recreation Commission, to Charles Knabusch, Chair, Michigan Natural Resources Trust Fund, thanking the Board for approval of an area of land 221' x 197' at the Northeast corner of the William H. Haithco Recreation Area for the location of a cellular tower. The County was to reimburse the Michigan Natural Resources Trust Fund $21,525 which presented 75% of the fair market value of the land.

According to an article with accompanying pictures in the February 22, 2000 Saginaw News, the lake at William H. Haithco Recreation Area was the location for the inaugural Polar Bear Plunge in Saginaw County, sponsored by the Michigan Law Enforcement Torch Run. The dip into icy waters raised more than $6,000 for Special Olympics Michigan. An article in the Metro Section of the Saginaw News of July 9, 2000 describes the benefits to be derived if a 0.1618-mill property tax increase is approved by voters. Tax revenues partially support the William H. Haithco Recreation Area, the Imerman Memorial Park, the Price Nature Center, and Ringwood Forest, and would provide a year-round ranger to patrol the parks.

The Tri-City Amateur Boat Builders sponsored the third annual Great Lakes Small Craft Symposium at Haithco Recreation area in August, 2000, according to the Saginaw News of August 21, 2000.

LAKE HAITHCO

Staff party

HAITHCO Staff PARTY

GREAT LAKES SMALL CRAFT SYMPOSIUM

HAITHCO RECREATION AREA
LAKE HAITHCO: SHARI & ANNMARIE

Alumni Pictures

**University of Michigan Alumni Get together
Left to right: Fred Waller,D. Bob Linton, Herman
Curtis,Dean Kenyon, Bill Haithco and Dick Banaos**

While Martin Luther King Jr. dreamed of a better life for this country's African Americans, mid-Michigan folks such as, from the top, Claudine "Mommy" Wicks, William Haithco and Ruben Daniels made those dreams come true.

William H. Haithco—Lending your name to a public institution is nothing new to many of Saginaw's community leaders.

But in Haithco's case, there's a neat twist to the story. The Saginaw pharmacist rolled up his sleeves and actually helped give birth to the 71-acre Saginaw Township park, tucked against Interstate 675 between Schust and McCarty.

And you might find him still, on his knees, planting flowers around the lake-front perimeter.

A member of the Arthur Hill High School class of 1940, Haithco said his mother "forced" him to attend college, but he's made the most of his education ever since.

His community activities, which include founding the Saginaw County Parks and Recreation Commission and serving as president of the University of Michigan College of Pharmacy Alumni Board of Governors, earned him recognition as an honored alumnus at Arthur Hill in 1991 and the U.S. Pharmacist/Searle Service to the Community Award in November of 1994.

And they named a park after him.

"I never told myself it wouldn't get done, because I'm an optimist. It's going to happen. It is happening," Haithco said in 1991.

7

Friends

The Bolfs

Rudy Bolf is Czech and his wife is German. Their daughter Nicola was little and Rudy's mother would tell Nicola when she asked what nationality she was that she was Czech. Bonnie would tell Nicola that she was German and then that would start the whole chain reaction. Nicola would salute like a German and Rudy's mother would say "Heil Hitler." Bonnie would say, "That's not right" to Nicola and she would then start in on Rudy's mother and say that she wasn't Czech but that she was German. The kidding went back and forth.

Nicola, Rudy and Bill Rose Bowl 1992

Nicola, Rudy and Bill

In May 1991, I was honored to become the 1991 Arthur Hill Honor Alumnus. Since that time, I have been invited to the Honors Dinner every year to honor that year's honor alumna. The 1994 Arthur Hill High School Honor Alumnus was Doug Peacock, who had graduated in 1960. Doug's underdog instincts have lead him on a wilderness odyssey through grizzly bear county that stretched over a quarter century. Doug spent much of his adult life living with the wild grizzly bears in the backcountry of Yellowstone and Glacier National Parks.

In 1990, Doug wrote a book titled "Grizzly Years: In Search of the American Wilderness." During our conversations, he mentioned he had recently returned from Belize, Central America, where he spent much time with the pandas, jaguars, and the grizzlies. At this point, I mentioned my hobby of collecting old marbles. I asked if he could find me some old marbles of the agate type. Doug had corresponded previously two to three times from Tucson, and then after he moved to Montana. In one of his cards he referred to the agates as "petrified wood". The mail lady came today (August 9, 2000) and brought a box from Doug containing the ingredients Doug has mentioned in his letter. Doug Peacock is white and we get along very well.

ell.

406 222 9792
2

Dear Bill,

Jan. 2002

I apologize for being such a lousy correspondent. I moved up here after my divorce - death of my father. It was rough for a while.

I was back in Saginaw, Bay City this May, saw the park on the river and visited the Shiawassee Bird Refuge. It was a wonderful revisit. Saw all my aunts + uncles and said goodbye to my dad's youngest brother who died last month.

My health is pretty good. I live at the edge of the Absaroka Wilderness overlooking a great valley 40 miles N of Yellowstone Park.

It never occurred to me I didn't have to come up with finished marbles instead of raw materials, which I run across all the time. Here's a sample, more to come. Looking Glass Rock, Blue Sul, UT; ② agate pebble (east SW AZ; ③ Brushy Basin chert, Bluff UT ④ _____ ⑤ quartzite, boulder, MT ⑥ Petrified wood, Gallatin Mts MT ⑦ chalcedony, Yellowstone, ⑧ Dacite? Yellowstone and ⑨ Obsidian from Obsidian Cliff, Yellowstone.

I live here now + won't be so hard to find.

your friend + admirer,

Doug Peacock

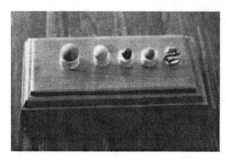

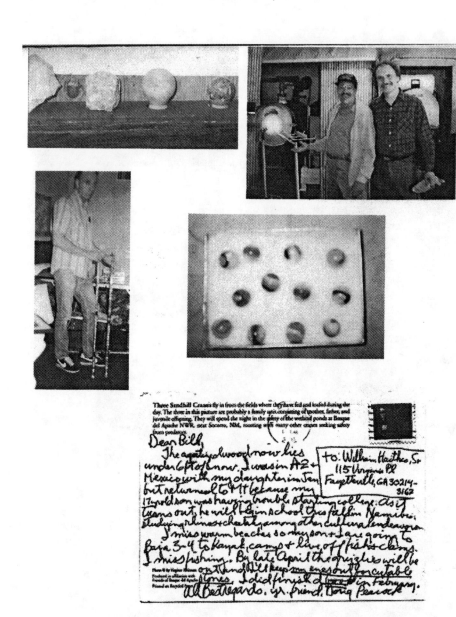

The Sturms

Frankenmuth, Michigan, is a small city southeast of Saginaw, Michigan. In June 1996, a tornado stuck Frankenmuth. The first place it hit was the farm property of the Sturms/Webbers southwest of the corner of Tuscola Road and Dehmel

Road. The corncrib was hit first and they have not found it yet. Its place of impact was west of Dehmel Road, along the Cass River. My pharmacist friend Dick Sturm and his wife Ginny owned the property where the tornado had its greatest impact. The land is just north of the house and north of the Cass River. This was the site of the old barn and farm that had been in the Webber Family for years. The silo and stainless steel roof on the barn were destroyed. Inside of the barn were many old farm tools and equipment. In the basement of the barn were hand hewn oak beams. These beams were from 12 to 31 feet in length and were about 12 inches square … and heavy.

Dick Sturm was my pharmacist friend for 20 years and when I heard of the tornado, I tried to call Dick and Ginny with no success. I then called Dick's mother, Eleanor Sturm, and she informed me all of the family were all right but they had no telephone service. Dick and Jim Webber, his brother-in-law, were organizing some friends from Frankenmuth to help clean up and take down. Jim Webber and his daughter, Dr. Webber and her husband Tim Coughlin, Dick and I, and three of Jim's friends first tore the tin roof off the shed and barn and then started to remove the 480 bails of hay and straw that was standing. Jim recalled the last farming was probably done around 1983. I worked every day for seven days helping in the cleanup. There was a cement basement in the barn that housed an old wagon and other old equipment. There were old hand-hewn oak posts ranging from 6 to 32 feet in length that were probably cut around 1883 and never were used in construction. Even the pegs ("nails") were hand hewn of wood! I have one or two as souvenirs in my antiques. There were 112 of these 12-inch square timbers and no place to put them. Jim Webber asked me to find someone who could use these valuable timbers.

After the July meeting of the Saginaw County Parks and Recreation Commission, I asked Jim Blashka if he could use these timbers and after the meeting I took Blashka out to Frankenmuth to see the "catch". I knew Hartley needed some repairs and new construction. Jim said he could use the timbers and some of the old hardwood lumber that had never seen such things as nails.

Now we have to find a way to get them to St. Charles (Michigan) that is some 23 miles away. Jim sent two men from the St. Charles area that came with a pick-up truck and small trailer and because the trailer was borrowed and only held three to five timbers, this phase was appreciated but bogged down. Tom Tilot of the Saginaw Board of Education said to me "Bill, why not use the Career Opportunities Center? They have all the equipment you could need." This plan never reached fruition.

I stopped to talk to my dear friends the Rhode Brothers, and Joe and I drove out to Frankenmuth one morning to assess the project needs: one or two trailers, one backhoe, one front-end loader, one or two trucks, one tractor and some man-power. This never got off the ground. Now it was getting very near snow time and the Sturms, Webbers, and Haithco became a little concerned about the snow causing harm to the wood!

In November, I took Harold McKellar to Ann Arbor to a Michigan football game. During our football stadium dialogue, I mentioned my interest in the 6630 Dehmel Road site. He mentioned he had a friend who might be able to help me. After the football game, we returned to Saginaw and went directly to Arthur Hill High School for the Fordney Club football game. There I met Dave McMath of the McMath Masonry Company and he volunteered to be a major part of the "tornado operation".

I got Dick to leave the tractor outside the barn and I helped Dave as he ran the tractor. We moved all the timbers and boards to Hartley in one day with Mac's help and two truck drivers with trailers and Dave. From here I let Dave and Jim Beaver run their venture!

Now, I wonder when the history of Hartley Outdoor Education Center and the History of Frankenmuth are printed and read, will the name of Bill Haithco, a black man and the black pharmacist, be listed as the designer-perpetrator of this venture, and included as an integral part of history??

8

Recognition and Awards

My Life and the Eclectic Mix of People

My life is surrounded by a number of awards and honors.

On July 1, 1970, I received the A.H. Robins Bowl of Hygeia Award, which is awarded to one pharmacist in each state and Puerto Rico for Outstanding Community Service in Pharmacy. I was the recipient of the award for the State of Michigan in 1970 at our summer convention at Boyne Mountain resort. What an experience, with the award not being announced until the time of the award. There were people following me around for three days trying to make sure I did not leave the convention before the meeting of the House of Delegates. At every convention since 1970, my name is mentioned as the new recipient is announced! The award is now given by the Wyeth-Robins Company. My picture appeared in TIME magazine.

In 1972, Dale Schultz, Director of Pharmacy, asked me to join his staff in the pharmacy at Saginaw General Hospital, and the same year I was asked to serve on the Board of Directors of the Saginaw General Credit Union. I served as President of the Credit Union for ten years. During the ten years, we moved our office from Anderson Hall to the upstairs of Brenske Plumbing and Heating across from Clark's Drugs, on West Genesee, to the Secretary of State office behind the Court Street Theater, to the present branch office at 2172 Hemmeter, and finally to the new main office at 1430 N. Michigan in June 1990.

The Saginaw Medical Federal Credit Union was chartered in 1971, and at this writing of this autobiography, has 10,500 members and assets of $45 million. Its field of membership includes health care employees and their families. I was Chairperson of the Board of Directors during the building of the new office at 1430 N. Michigan, but for some multicultural adversity reason, my title never appeared on the plaque placed in the entrance with the chrome-plated shovel. Credit Union service is very educational and provides a great exposure to the financial industry and its operation.

My service to the Credit Union lasted for 25 years, ten of which were as president of the Board of Directors of the Saginaw Medical Federal Credit Union. On October 21, 1978, I was awarded the Credit Union Person of the Year of the Saginaw Chapter and on June 1, 1979, I was awarded the Ronald L. Wilde Memorial Award as Michigan's Credit Union Person of the Year, awarded by the Michigan Credit Union Foundation. This award consisted of a bronze plaque and a scholarship award of $500 to the University of my choice. I chose the College of Pharmacy of the University of Michigan. I added $100 out-of-pocket to this award, as the Outstanding Student selected by the Board of Admissions of the University was determined to be three students, and my personal contribution would allow each student to receive $200.00.

For one year, I served as president of the Saginaw Chapter of Credit Unions, consisting of 23 credit unions. This position was very politically interesting, to say the least!

There were three women at my credit union that did not realize that I knew what "eye contact" was. Whenever one of them would see me outside the work place, they were very embarrassed to be seen speaking (saying hello) to me in public. I once said, "If you are blonde and we meet in the market, go and hide your head amongst a bunch of cauliflower so you will not be noticed". Then I would ask, "If I should happen to see you in your car overturned in a ditch of water, what should I do?"

Volunteering has been a way of life for me. I have been recognized for my commitment to volunteering in, the Michigan Credit Union League Contact Magazine of October 1983, as well as by the American Lung Association of Michigan, and the Saginaw News. "When someone asks me to serve in a volunteer capacity I feel a great need to do so ... People volunteer because they want to serve, because they want to do something positive for their communities. Volunteers are probably the most dedicated people there are."

In 1984, I received a Special Award from the Michigan Recreation and Parks Association for advocating and supporting parks and recreation in the state of Michigan.

In 1986, I was awarded the Pharmacist of the Year Award from the Saginaw County Pharmacist Association.

In 1986, I was awarded the Michigan Pharmacist Hall of Honor Award.

In 1988 I was awarded the J. C. Penney Golden Rule Award for Voluntary Service to the Community. This was the first year this award was given in Saginaw and it included a cash award of $1,000.00, which was given to the Saginaw County Parks Fund.

In 1991, I received the American Lung Association of Michigan Volunteer Recognition Award. I served on this board for 10 years before having my open heart surgery in 1998. In 1991, I also received the Gordon F. Goyette, Jr., Humanitarian Award, presented by the Wayne County Pharmacists Association. This was the first year for this award by the Wayne County (Michigan) Pharmacists Association and the Wayne State University Pharmacy School.

In May 1991, I was chosen as the 1991 Arthur Hill High School Honor Alumnus and I have served on this "committee" ever since.

It is interesting to note the stereotyping and categorizing white people use very conveniently. Note the letter from Jerry Nissley dated May 9, 1991, honoring me as the Saginaw High School Honor Alumnus when all news articles told of my being the 1991 Honor Alumnus of Arthur Hill High School! I graduated from Arthur Hill in 1940 and at that time in history there were two high schools in the public school system, Saginaw High School on the east side of the city and Arthur Hill High School on the west side. There were only seven black families living on the west side of Saginaw at that time. The great majority of black students attended Saginaw High and I guess Jerry thought I must have attended Saginaw High. Sorry, Jerry!

On August 1, 1994, in Las Vegas I received the National Outstanding Volunteer for Parks and Recreation Award presented by the National Association of Parks and Recreation Officials. This award meant much to me as my daughter Shari met me in Vegas and was my guest.

The big surprise for us was the arrival of Bill and Ruth Patterson as Shari and I sat in the dining room waiting for the event to begin. We were waiting with Brian and Amy Barber when I looked up and saw Ruth and Bill entering the dining room. Bill is a pharmacist from Oxford, Michigan, one that I nominated for the Pharmacist of Michigan Executive Board in February 1984 at our state convention at the Hyatt Regency in Dearborn. In July 1989, at the Michigan Pharmacists Convention on Mackinaw Island, I was the Master of Ceremonies at the dinner honoring Bill Patterson as our new Pharmacist State President. I composed a video of Bill from birth up to the present ... great fun as I had all the people from Oxford, and Pharmacist Gary Hobbs and wife Pat from Merritt Island, Florida, in attendance also.

At the beginning of my presentation, I noted all the people from Oxford and I asked if there were any people left in Oxford. Someone amongst the 400 people present said, "Only the sick". I guess multicultural diversity really doesn't hurt as Bill Patterson had an aneurysm in April 1994 and he and Ruth made the Vegas ceremony on August 1, 1994.

Bill and Ruth made the Lake Haithco dedication in May of 1991 and have made our annual picnic at Lake Haithco every year since. These are the family members of the Bill and Ruth Pattersons: Rick and Pam Patterson; Mary Jo and Brad Bierworth; Terry and Brad Jacobsen; Jean and Tim Davidson; and Barb and Chris Kaiser.

The past three years the University of Michigan College of Pharmacy Dean Jim Richard and granddaughter Tiffany have also joined us. Jim was a classmate of Bill Patterson at the University of Michigan, class of 1955.

I was notified by Dawn Durham, R.Ph., that I had been selected to be the recipient of the U.S. Pharmadcist/Searle Service To The Community Award in November 1994. "Clearly your devotion to providing outstanding service to your community was evident in the nomination provided, and it is Searle's privilege to be apart of this recognition."

I was awarded the 2003 University of Michigan Alumni Association Distinguished Alumni Service Award. This award is presented annually to individuals "who have distinguished themselves by their service to the University and/or the Alumni Association. It is the highest honor that the Alumni Association can bestow upon a member of the alumni body."

The Michigan Pharmacists Association named me Pharmacist of the Year for 2003. This award is given to a pharmacist "who demonstrates professional excellence and exemplary service to the profession in advancing public health at either the state or local level and displays all the traits and characteristics of someone with a true commitment to advancing the pharmaceutical profession and public health."

NOTE: If God made any better Multicultural Diversifiers
He must have kept them to Himself!

On June 22, 1999, I was given the Resolution of Appreciation by the County Parks and Recreation Saginaw County Board of Commissioners at its meeting at the Saginaw Governmental Center.

At this meeting, Dick Mallette, a member of the County Parks and Recreation Commission and also a member of the Saginaw County Parks and Recreation Commission, made the award and no other members of the Parks and Recreation Commission were present (I missed two meetings in thirty years).

RESOLUTION OF APPRECIATION
Presented To:
WILLIAM H. HAITHCO

- **WHEREAS,** The Saginaw County Parks and Recreation Commission was officially established by the Board of Supervisors in September 1969. Shortly thereafter, William H. Haithco was appointed as a member, and has been affiliated with the Commission for nearly thirty years hence; and,

- **WHEREAS,** William H. Haithco, or "Bill" as he is known by his friends and constituents has a gift for bringing people together, and a knack for achieving positive results; and,

- **WHEREAS,** Bill is known for being a "hands on" person. If there is a job to be done, you can always count on his help. Bill is also very well known for his humor. Whatever the situation might be, Bill has a funny story or antidote to coincide; and,

- **WHEREAS,** Upon his retirement from his responsibilities as a member and long time Chairman of the Saginaw County Parks & Recreation Commission, Bill brings to a close an outstanding career; and,

- **WHEREAS,** The belief in the need for a community to have recreational opportunities is evident and led Bill to achieve great success. His energies and abilities have proven invaluable to the Saginaw County Parks Commission and the void he leaves will be deeply felt; and,

- **WHEREAS,** It will come as no surprise to those who know Bill best, to learn that his retirement will not herald the end of his community involvement. We are confident that wherever he goes, others will be the beneficiary of his efforts.

- **NOW THEREFORE, BE IT RESOLVED,** That tribute be hereby accorded to Mr. William Haithco as he retires from his responsibilities with the Saginaw County Parks & Recreation Commission; and,

- **BE IT FURTHER RESOLVED,** That a copy of this resolution be spread upon the minutes of this meeting so that future generations will be appreciative of the lasting contributions of Mr. William H. Haithco.

Respectfully,
SAGINAW COUNTY BOARD OF COMMISSIONERS
Robert L. Fish, Chair
Roland G. Niederstadt. Clerk

Acquisition of land for the Saginaw Valley Rail Trail was completed in the fall of 1999. The Rail-Trail runs from Lumberjack Park in St. Charles to Paine Junction in James Township in Saginaw County. It incorporates a number of natural features including eight bridges over various rivers and creeks, The Shiawassee State Game Area, and many wetlands areas.

To honor long-time Saginaw County Parks and Recreation Commission Chairman William Haithco, a bronze plaque bearing his likeness is on display at the William H. Haithco Recreation Area.

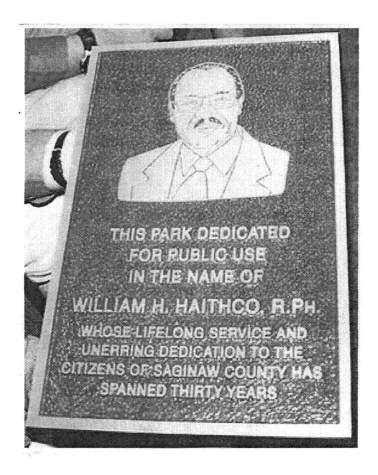

At its October 1983 meeting, the Pharmacy Alumni Society Board of Governors elected as its new chairman William H. Haithco, Sr., '52 B.S. Pharm. Mr. Haithco, pharmacist at Saginaw General Hospital, has been a member of the board since its inception in 1977, and replaced outgoing board president Peter A. Reilly, '66 B.S. Pharm.

In 2003 The University of Michigan recognized the long-time loyalty and distinction William H. Haithco's achievements brought his alma mater when the Alumni Association presented him with the Distinguished Alumni Service Award, the highest honor the Association can confer.

The Membership Award for 50 years of service was awarded to William H. Haithco during the Michigan Pharmacists Association Banquet in 2004.

William H. Haithco was included among the Winners of the U.S. Pharmacist/Searle Service to the Community Award, which recognizes pharmacists who have contributed their expertise, time and effort to provide programs and services of distinct benefit to the community. He never left his birthplace of Saginaw, Michigan, and is on the map, literally. Among the five parks that he helped develop were the William H. Haithco Recreation Area and Lake Haithco.

William H. Haithco knew there was a great need to develop—and fund—county parks. He formed the Saginaw County Parks Fund so local residents could help fund and provide increased recreational facilities and programs in the county. He credits the Saginaw Community Foundation for making his dream for county parks possible.

William H. Haithco, owner of Haithco Prescription Pharmacy for 14 years was awarded the National Association of County Parks & Recreations Officials (NACPRO) Outstanding Volunteer Award for 1994. In 1969 he founded the Saginaw County Parks & Recreation Commission, and became chairman in 1972. The William H. Haithco Recreation Area was created in his honor in 1991.

"What a man does for himself dies with him. What he does for others will live forever." These words were a constant source of inspiration for Bill Haithco. For him, volunteering was a way of life. He served on numerous volunteer boards, commissions and advisory groups. He admits that volunteering is "in his blood". People volunteer because they want to serve, because they want to do something positive for their communities, he says. "Volunteers are probably the most dedicated people there are."

A Saginaw County lake has been named in honor of recently retired Saginaw General Hospital Pharmacist Bill Haithco in recognition of his service as Chairman of the Saginaw County Parks Commission.

Activities/Community Involvement

Past President, Saginaw Area Pharmacists Association, Pharmacist of the Year, 1987

President, Saginaw Medical Federal Credit Union Board of Directors, 10 years

Founder, Saginaw County Parks Funds, a Donor Advised Fund under the Saginaw Community Foundation.

Chairperson, Saginaw County Parks & Recreation Commission

District Director, Michigan Pharmacists Political Action Committee for 26 years

Chairperson, Saginaw County Parks Fund Advisory Council

Member, Executive Committee, Saginaw Chapter of Credit Unions

Member, Delta College Committee of "100"

Member, Saginaw Future Committee that tries to lay out future directions the county must follow.

Member, Delta College/Jacobson's Possible Dream Scholarship Committee

Treasurer, Dispute Resolution Committee of Saginaw County

(Saginaw County Bar Assn.)

Member, American Lung Association of Michigan Board of Directors

Member, Saginaw Area Pharmacists

Member, University of Michigan Club of Saginaw

Member, Michigan State University Club of Saginaw

Member, Michigan Pharmacists Association,

Member, American Society of Hospital Pharmacists Council on Legal & Public Affairs

Awards

- Bowl of Hygeia Award, A. H. Robins Company
- Credit Union Person of the Year, Saginaw Chapter
- Michigan Credit Union Person of the Year, Ronald L. Wilde Memorial Award.
- Consisted of $500 scholarship to college of choice. I chose the College of Pharmacy of the University of Michigan and added $100 to the award to make $600, as the University chose to give it to three pharmacy recipients (total award $200 per student)
- Special Award, Michigan Recreation & Parks Association for
- Advocating and Supporting Parks & Recreation in the State of Michigan
- Pharmacist of the Year, Saginaw County Pharmacist Association
- Michigan Pharmacists Association Hall of Honor Award
- JC Penney Golden Rule Award for Voluntary Service to the Community. The award included $1,000, which was given to the Saginaw County Parks Fund
- American Lung Association of Michigan Volunteer Recognition Award
- Gordon F. Goyette, Jr., Humanitarian Award, presented by Wayne County Pharmacists Association
- Arthur Hill High School Honor Alumnus
- National Outstanding Volunteer for Parks & Recreation Award presented by National Association of Parks & Recreation Officials
- U.S. Pharmacist/Searle Service to the Community Award
- Saginaw County Board of Commissioners, Resolution of Appreciation for Community Service
- Michigan Pharmacist of the Year
- University of Michigan Alumni Association Distinguished Alumni Service Award

Professional Career

Owned Haithco Prescription Pharmacy for 14 years
Pharmacist, Saginaw General Hospital for 17 years

Other Volunteer Activities

Big Brothers and Big Sisters, 2 years
Mayor's Committee of Concern, Henry G. Marsh, Mayor
Junior Achievement of Saginaw, 2 years
East Central Michigan Health Systems Agency, 6 years, President, 3 years
Selective Service Board #339, 1968–71
Board of Directors, Saginaw Model Cities Involvement Corporation
Governor's Comprehensive Health Planning Advisory Council, 1969–71;
Chairperson of the Legislative Review Committee
Charter Member, Saginaw Breakfast Optimist Club, President for 1 term
Northern Michigan Area Health Education Center, Member/Vice President, 1984–90
National President, University of Michigan College of Pharmacy Alumni Board of Governors, 1981–84
National Vice President, Michigan State University College of Natural Science Board of Directors, 1981–86

Education and Military Service

Upon graduation from Arthur Hill High School, I spent time at Bay City Junior College just prior to a stint in the U.S. Air Force.
Michigan State University
East Lansing, Michigan
Bachelor of Science, Physiology & Pharmacology

University of Michigan
Ann Arbor, Michigan
Bachelor of Science, Pharmacy

Friends Who Make my Life Enjoyable
Alaska

A little later we will be at the face of Alaska's most active tidewater glacier, the Columbia. The face of the Columbia is two and one-half miles wide and towers 260 feet above the water line. Considered to be one of the most photogenic glaciers on the Alaska coast, it will regularly heave icebergs the size of small buildings into the sound. Next we see the hart of the strikingly beautiful Fjord where we see many glaciers, such as the Harvard, Yale, Vassar, Wellesley, and Radcliff. The Harriman Expedition named these glaciers in 1899 for the colleges that supported the expedition's survey of the area.

The next morning at 6 a.m., the ship docked at Whittier where debarkation took place, and we traveled from Whittier to Anchorage by rail and motor coach, along the Turn Again Arm of the Cook Inlet. We arrived in Anchorage about 11:15 a.m. in time to board our plane for Fairbanks about 1:15 a.m. The airlines scheduled to fly us to Fairbanks was a small airline based in Florida. This airline did not show up and we were placed in a substitute plane, which would not contain all of us on our charter flight. So I had to wait for another plane, a twelve-passenger plane that would fly a few others and me to Fairbanks. Yes, "five feet two, eyes of blue" little Bonnie stood up in righteous indignation to protest this separation of our group. After being assured that Bill Haithco would be landing in Fairbanks only twenty to thirty minutes after the main flight had landed, our "flight" pattern proceeded. You see, Bonnie and Mili may have had different complexions but similar compassion. Yes, it does take a whole community to raise a child. The butcher, the baker, the candlestick maker, the Czech, the German, the black, the English, the Italian, the French, the teach, and Humpty Uppity. WE all have fun. Try it! It doesn't hurt. It helps.

Immediately on our arrival in Fairbanks, we were taken to the riverboat "Discovery" which returned at 6:00 p.m. We spent the night in Fairbanks at the Regency Hotel. Sunday morning, July 27, we left the hotel for a drive through the city of Fairbanks to visit the University of Alaska Museum and make a few stops in Fairbanks for gift buying and sight seeing. It was at a gift shop that the Attorneys Weisman from Fort Wayne (Indiana) decided to "speak" and be sociable. It was this couple and their friends from Indiana travel group that had great difficulty trying to understand what I was doing in our group and who was that beautiful blond in our group of size. Every morning as I was standing at the rail observing the scenery and the sun rise, they could get closer and closer to me in a state of sheer curiosity.

Our train for the ride through Denali national Park was the "Midnight Sun Express". Brunch and drinks were served in the superdome of the train (for a fee). Denali national Park is 6 million acres and we were fortunate to see caribou in the fireweed, Dall sheep at a distance, the top-secret radar detection station, Musher Mary Shields and her dogs and her salmon ladder, Captain Binkley, and Mt. McKinley from 40 miles away.

Worthy of note while on the riverboat Discovery was the "divide", where the CHENA and TENANA rivers intersect at a ninety-degree angel. The Chena River is dark muddy and the Tenana River is a bluish green. This trip through the Denali Park was very interesting and we arrived at our park hotel, the McKinley Chalet, at about 10 p.m. for the evening.

The next morning at 8:30 a.m., we had our luggage set outside our room and we just roamed around until time to leave on the Midnight Sun Express train at 1:30 p.m. Our train arrived in Anchorage about 8:30 p.m. and we roamed around and did a little shopping. I managed to buy a pair of house slippers made from doeskin and seal hair by some Alaskan native at $95.00 a pair. The cruise was fantastic and I decided to take our party out for dinner on this our last night in Alaska. So I took them to the Kayak Club down at the oceanfront for an Alaskan King Crab Dinner that was fabulous. We had decided to send some king crab legs back to Michigan for our mutual friends Bruce and Connie Booth to pick up at the airport. WE decided to walk back to the address we found in the newspaper for wholesale seafood. As we walked, the wind became stronger and we finally came to two couples washing their new car. I guess we looked like tourists … lost. One gentleman asked where we were from and I answered "down below", Michigan. He then asked what we were looking for and I answered, "Seafood, King Crab legs". We wanted to send some back to Michigan for a party. He then proceeded to tell us the king crab legs were caught in Alaska, then shipped to Seattle, Washington, for processing then back to Anchorage for ale. He aid we would get them cheaper in Michigan. So we thanked him and walked on. We spent the night at Sheffield Anchorage and flew back to Seattle on Wednesday, July 30, the back to Detroit from there.

What a beautiful cruise. Seeing the EXPO 86, Vancouver, Ketchikan, Skagway, Juneau, Whittier, Anchorage, Chilkoot Trail, taking the helicopter ride to the Mendenhall Glacier, walking on the glacier, watching the captain's crew drop a boat in the ocean to cut a large block of ice from the iceberg, bring the ice back into the ship, and carve it into a large rabbit for display at the midnight "snack", the Alaskan Musher and her dog, the Chena and Teanan Rivers joining, the

Denali national Park, the wildlife and salmon, the cultural atmosphere of Fairbanks.

What a display of multicultural diversity that all on the cruise envied. Try it sometime! I once read an article in Reader's Digest that went as follows "Once upon a time, there was a young man who wanted to become a great writer. 'I want to write things the whole world will read,' he declared. Stuff that will elicit strong emotions from people in very walk of life. I ant my writing to make them scream, cry, howl in pain and anger.' He now lives happily ever after in Redman, Washington, writing error messages for Microsoft." Contributed by Richard A. Wright.

ALASKAN CRUISE

BONNIE   NICOLA   D.L.   B.O

MISTY FJORD

Caribou "FIREWEED" at DENALI

CREEK STREET "RED LIGHT"

RONNIE & NICCI

Caribbean Cruise

In 1984, Rudy Bolf, a fellow pharmacist, invited me to go with them for seven days on my FIRST vacation of my life. I accepted, and I joined them for the Caribbean Cruise on the Cunard Princess. It was nice, as I learned to "relax". My roommate was a world traveler and could NOT speak any English. One night he left the water in the cabin running all night while he and his travel mates partied. There was water into the hallway! But the cruise liner crew took up the rugs and cleared away the water.

It was on this trip I collected some Jalapeno Hot Peppers that I brought back … in a shirt … and tried to grow.

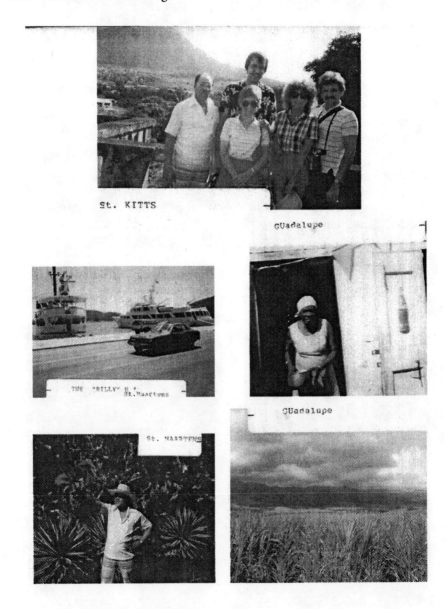

St. KITTS

GUadalupe

THE "BILLY" H.
St. Maartens

St. MAARTENS

GUadalupe

Deep Sea Fishing—Gulf of Mexico

For three or four years, Tony Miller, a former roommate of my son Billy, at Kalamazoo College, ran a fishing trip at Orange Beach, Alabama. Usually Shari and I drove down and joined the 10-member group in a large cottage in Orange Beach. We would leave at 3:00 a.m. for a one-day fishing trip for Red Snapper plus! We returned home on Sunday morning. Quite an experience in the 100-foot-plus boat!

Mackinaw Island

For four or five years, Rudy and Bonnie Bolf sponsored a trip to mackinaw Island where about 23 of us would rent the Whole Pontiac Lodge on the Island for two days of cross county skiing. Usually, their daughter Milk would bring her friends and we would party. The group consisted of Pharmacists, Pharmacy Technicians, Nurses, etc. and families.

Usually the people who own the Pontiac Lodge would open their restaurant net door for two evening meals.

We all drove to mackinaw and then flew across to the Island. One year we could not fly so they gave us a boat to ride over!

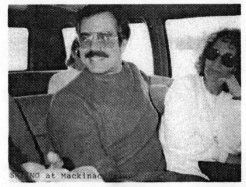

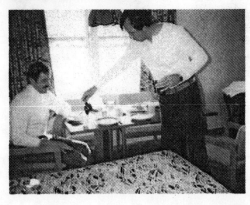

978-0-595-43865-5
0-595-43865-2

Printed in the United States
88700LV00003B/345/A

9 780595 438655